Self-Hypnosis
Creating Your Own Destiny

By Henry Leo Bolduc

A.R.E.® PRESS • VIRGINIA BEACH • VIRGINIA

ISBN 87604-160-8

Printed in the U.S.A.

Contents

Chapter Ten
Cycles for Touching a Larger Consciousness

Acknowledgments

I am profoundly appreciative of the many people whose love and generosity have helped make this book possible. I am especially grateful to Ann Phelan Adams, Diane Davidson Cayce, Sharon Fowler, Geraldine McDowell, George Parker, and Eileen Rota Wirtanen for their help with the self-hypnosis programs or "cycles." For technical assistance, I am indebted to Elwood Babbitt, Elmer M. Cranton, M.D., and Leon Szwabowski, D.C. I thank Susie Bell, Jerry Kandies, and Lenora Rose for their hours of typing and clerical work. A very special thank you to Dr. Mark Thurston, my editor, and to the literally hundreds of people who have worked with and evaluated these cycles.

A Note to the Reader

Self-Hypnosis: Creating Your Own Destiny is a self-help book. It does not intend to treat, diagnose, prescribe or offer medical advice. If you have a health problem or wish to begin any health program, you should first consult your family health practitioner.

Introduction

Henry Bolduc has written a practical and immediately applicable book on an often misunderstood topic. As both a trained professional hypnotist and serious student of the Edgar Cayce readings, he is able to show us step-by-step procedures for using self-hypnosis in personal change. The techniques found in this book will give you powerful tools toward the realization of your spiritual, mental, and physical ideals.

The topic of hypnosis is a controversial one, whether we are speaking of clinical hypnosis administered by a health care professional or self-hypnosis. There has always been a mystique surrounding hypnosis, a sense of mystery that is both intriguing and frightening. This book can help dispel much of that fear. Especially in the area of self-hypnosis, which is the exclusive focus of this book's presentation, you will discover how *you* are in control of those forces of change stimulated by hypnosis techniques and principles. As long as the hypnotic programs (or "cycles," as they are called in this book) are consistent with your highest ideals, there is nothing to fear from this approach to working with your subconscious mind. In fact, this book teaches you how to develop a cooperative relationship with your inner self, a relationship which is likely to lead to healing and greater fulfillment in your life.

The term "hypnosis" originated with the work of a Scottish surgeon, James Braid, working in the 1840s, and it comes from the Greek root word *hypnos* (meaning sleep). It refers to a state of consciousness that in many ways is like sleep, but allows a variety of mental and behavioral responses to stimulation. In response to suggestions to the unconscious, even memory patterns and the awareness of self may be changed.

When hypnotized by someone else, the subject may appear to relinquish his or her own will—seeing, feeling, smelling, and tasting in accordance with the suggestions given. Depending upon the depth of the hypnotic state and the strength of the suggestions, the subject may even accept as being real certain distortions of memory and perception offered by the hypnotist.

Hypnotic techniques have been used for thousands of years. Certain healing therapies conducted by priests in ancient Egypt, Greece, and China greatly resemble current hypnosis practices. The modern rediscovery of hypnosis is generally attributed to Dr. Franz Mesmer (1734-1815). An Austrian physician working in Vienna and Paris in the late 1700s, he discovered that some ailing people obtained relief when magnets were brought near their bodies. Patients were instructed to sit as a group around an open container of water in which magnetized metal bars were visible. Occasionally, a patient would seem to fall into a sleeplike state and, soon after regaining consciousness, be much improved or even fully cured. Later, Mesmer discovered that the magnets were unnecessary. He found that results could also be obtained in some cases simply by touching the patient or by touching the water before the patient drank it. To his mind, the touching of the water "magnetized it." Mesmer theorized that he and other people had "animal magnetism"—that they had access to a kind of mysterious "fluid" which was stored within and could be transferred to others and thus effect a healing. Soon there were over 100 groups of people in France performing similar healings; they were called the Society of Harmony.

A protégé of Mesmer, named Chastenet de Puységur, felt that he, too, had this power of "animal magnetism" and magnetized a tree on his property. Peasants living nearby who came in contact with this tree reported obtaining relief from a variety of ailments. However, Puységur soon found that it was unnecessary for people seeking a cure to fall into the convulsive-like fits which often characterized Mesmer's work (and can still be seen in the present at some charismatic healing services). Using a technique in many ways similar to modern hypnosis, he demonstrated that beneficial results could be obtained simply by talking to the patient.

These developments caused such a stir in Europe that a special investigative committee was appointed in Paris to study the new phenomenon. Benjamin Franklin and Dr. Joseph Guillotin were among those serving on this committee. Their conclusion was that no mysterious magnetic "fluid" exists, and, whereas some of the remarkable cures effected by Mesmer and his followers could not be denied, the committee attributed the healings to "mere imagination." Largely because of the findings of this committee, hypnosis fell into disrepute and further scientific investigation was neglected.

In the early decades of the 19th century, mesmeric techniques continued to be practiced by some. It was Dr. James Braid who not only gave us the modern term *hypnosis* but from his hospital work also reached a critical insight about the nature of hypnotic technique. While agreeing that no magnetic fluid was involved in the process, he reaffirmed that something significantly therapeutic was involved. In an effort to separate this phenomenon from theories of animal magnetism, he asserted that the concentration of attention in a single focus was the major factor in stimulating the hypnotic effect.

The late 19th century saw a reawakening of great interest in hypnosis. The Austrian physician, Sigmund Freud, learned of the techniques during visits to France and was impressed by the possibilities of hypnosis for treating neurotic disorders. In his own practice he began to use hypnosis to help some of his patients remember disturbing events from the past. As his system of psychoanalysis began to take shape, however, he rejected deepstate hypnosis in favor of the technique of relaxed-level free association. This may have been at least partly due to difficulties he encountered in hypnotizing certain patients.

In the 20th century there has been an impressive amount of experimental research with this hypnotic phenomenon; however, there is no one theory that is universally accepted by practitioners. Broadly speaking, there are two camps among professionals who work with hypnosis.

On the one hand are those who feel that hypnosis is a distinct altered state of consciousness, in many ways resembling sleep. In this altered state of awareness the subject responds to suggestion in a rather automatic and noncritical fashion. The focus with this theory is the proposed reality of altered states of consciousness.

On the other hand are those who feel that it is unnecessary to theorize about other states of consciousness in order to explain the workings of hypnosis. People operating from this perspective stress that behavior during hypnotic episodes can usually be explained in terms of social or interpersonal dynamics and learned behavior. As examples, they point to the placebo effect, which is demonstrated when a patient obtains relief from a neutral or inert pill given by a doctor simply because the patient has expectations that the physician's remedy will work. Another example from this point of view would be the ease with which a child or impressionable student will change his or her way of thinking about an issue to match that of an admired parent or teacher. According to this second theory, hypnotic responses are therefore seen as the mere result of interpersonal influences and subtle kinds of learning which don't require the concept of altered consciousness.

The perspective of hypnosis which we find in the Edgar Cayce readings seems to favor the first theory. Although there is research which supports the second point of view, there is clear, clinical evidence that physiological changes in the nervous system occur during hypnosis. The demonstrated reality of post-hypnotic suggestions (i.e., behaviors conducted even when the hypnotist may neither know nor be interested in the subject's later behavior) also indicates that something beyond merely interpersonal relationship influences are at work in hypnosis. Certainly if we are to consider the possibility of self-hypnosis techniques such as this book focuses upon, we must accept the first theory. The Edgar Cayce readings would seem to agree that hypnosis involves a distinct altered state of consciousness, which can admittedly be induced in an interpersonal relationship by a trained clinician, or it can be self-awakened.

What does research psychology tell us about the induction of the hypnotic state? One helpful ingredient is *belief* or acceptance on the part of the subject. Responsiveness is increased to the extent that the individual who is being hypnotized believes that it is possible. The depth of hypnotic effect is also enhanced to the extent that the patient feels that what will transpire during the hypnotic session is congruent with his or her "wishes." Another way of saying this, using language more familiar to the Edgar Cayce readings, is congruence with "ideals."

Research also shows that if appropriate preparations are taken, tape-recorded induction procedures may be just as effective as the "live" voice of an experienced hypnotist. This finding is especially significant in light of the procedures recommended in this book. The author will encourage you to make your own self-hypnosis tape recordings and to use the sound of your own voice as an induction.

As a further reassurance about self-control during hypnosis, research indicates that the hypnotic state cannot be induced against the individual's own desires or will. As previously stated, this places the control within the person himself who is experiencing the hypnotic state.

What does clinical research show about the nature of hypnotic suggestion itself? There are certain qualities of speech that seem to be especially beneficial to the process. Qualities of directness and simplicity—as well as insistent intensity—are often ascribed to effective wordings of suggestion. The use of vivid visual imagery—word pictures, which suggest specific images and invite the participation of the imaginative forces—is especially good. Direct commands are not as effective as a more gentle, implicit, or indicative form of speech. In other words, it's probably not the best hypnotic suggestion to give an order, such as "raise your arm." Instead, the hypnotic induction might more indirectly include wording in which it is suggested that the arm is feeling light, or that the arm feels as if it has helium-filled balloons attached to it, etc.

What kinds of results might we expect from hypnosis, either that conducted by a trained professional or that which is conducted by oneself? Research suggests that post-hypnotic suggestions are especially effective in the corrective treatment of strong habit patterns. You will find that many of the suggested hypnotic programs or "cycles" in this book are ones which deal with these kinds of self-limiting habit patterns that many of us encounter in daily life. In fact, research indicates that post-hypnotic suggestion is more effective in influencing this kind of habitual behavior than it is in influencing more straightforward, trivial tasks. However, for most of us, the need and desire to change ourselves relates not so much to simplistic behaviors in life, but, instead, to more ingrained subconscious habit patterns—habits of behavior, attitude or emotion—from which we hope to free ourselves. It is with these habit patterns that we endeavor to get assistance through hypnotic techniques.

In summary, then, scientific study has found that hypnotic induction requires little specific training and that often tape recordings are sufficient to induce the hypnotic state. Despite the simplicity there are, however, profoundly important issues related to the *process* of hypnosis. First is the personality of the person, including his or her ideals and motivations as well as expectations and hopes. And then, in those cases involving both a hypnotist and a client, there is the crucial factor of the interaction or interpersonal relationship between the two people.

In many ways, hypnosis is seen to be a powerful and yet neutral tool in its own right. Although little skill or training is needed to learn the induction of hypnosis, either in someone else or in one's self, serious self-study and practice are needed in order to use this powerful technique effectively. As a rule of thumb, many professional clinicians feel that hypnosis should never be employed by individuals who lack the skill and competence to deal with the same problems without using hypnosis. Assuming this is an advisable principle, what relevance does it have to the self-hypnotic approach described in this book? Most fundamentally, it probably says that we should not see self-hypnosis as some kind of magic incantation which will change us irrespective of ideals and personal desire. Hypnosis is not a way to avoid or short-circuit personal responsibility and application of will. Instead, the self-hypnotic techniques of this book are meant to assist you in making those changes in your own life toward which you are already prepared to work. In other words, we might say that certain hypnotic "cycles" from this book are likely to be more important and helpful to you than others. Most helpful will be the ones related to areas of your life where you are already prepared to use ideals, prayer, and will to create change.

The Edgar Cayce Readings on Hypnosis

With merely a quick reading of excerpts from the Cayce readings on hypnosis, we might at first feel that all that is offered is a collection of contradictory statements. On the one hand, there are instances where the readings strongly suggest that individuals use hypnosis in a therapeutic fashion. In other cases, individuals are warned against its use.

In one reading we find a statement reminiscent of the summary conclusion, stated above, from clinical research on hypnosis. Answering the question of a 46-year-old man who some 20 years earlier had experimented with his abilities as a hypnotist, the reading seems to suggest that hypnosis is a powerful technique which is neutral in and of itself but can be harnessed toward psychic and soul development if used with the ideals of service and healing others.

> Q-7. What is the significance, in my present state of development, of my power to administer hypnosis when I was a young man, 27 years ago?

> A-7. As has been indicated, this is a part of the development—through the experiences. As to apply same, as such things are a part of the psychic or soul development—this study; not as for self but for help and aid; so that directing in psychological suggestions will enable for self to apply same in the present—not to self advantageously so much, but as the *good* brings the good for *all*, it brings to others the help, to self the confidence, and the greater faith in the *Divine* within.
> 1497-1

Along a similar line of reasoning, the readings warn another individual, a 33-year-old man, not to get involved in hypnosis, largely because of the way his ego would become overly involved and distort the results. Haven't we all seen or heard of individuals who skillfully master techniques as hypnotists, and yet experience a kind of ego inflation related to the notoriety it generates or the control it gives over others?

> Q-3. Could good be derived for others and myself by my interest in and practice of self-hypnosis, or the general subject of hypnotism?

> A-3. This is far afield for this entity. There may be the interest, but we would not advise it for the entity itself. It may aid others. It is the desire to aid others, but

there is too much ego, too much I AM—if the I Am is
stressed in the correct emphasis—for hypnosis to be
applicable in the experience of the individual entity.

3348-1

Despite these cautions, there are many instances in
which the Cayce readings are very supportive of the use
of hypnosis. Let's look first at some of the examples from
the readings in which hypnosis *was* specifically recommended. Each excerpt will be introduced by a brief reference to the problem experienced by the person receiving
the reading.

Frequent headaches in a 45-year-old man (Edgar
Cayce himself). In this excerpt hypnosis itself is not
specifically recommended but suggestive therapeutics in
general is.

*Q-1. Mr. Cayce, what will relieve this body's head-
aches and what causes it?*

A-1. Suggestion to remove those conditions that
produce the headaches will relieve the condition in the
body, "that the circulation be so equalized as to remove
any strain on any portion of the body or not to overtax
the nervous system in any manner or form." The con-
gestion produces the headaches to this body by being
overtaxed through suggestion in the normal state, not
in the spiritual or soul state. The overtaxation comes to
the body in the normal and affects the action of the
forces that have to do with the psychical, spiritual or
soul forces of this body, see? 294-4

Addiction to alcohol in a 55-year-old man. Note
the reference in this passage to the purpose for hypnosis:
to help arouse the will of the individual to gain control of
the condition for himself.

In meeting the needs of the conditions in the present, as we find, it will require not only a desire for the
awakening of forces within self that may combat evil
influences in the inner life, but the maintaining of
those conditions in the body for the period that will allow *physically* the spiritual forces to exert themselves.

Either, then, through applications of subjugating the conscious mind through hypnosis or through those treatments that may be accorded in those places where both drink *and* sedatives may be taken *from* the body in such a manner that will allow the physical to exert itself. For, unless there is the arousing, under such conditions, for the *will* of the body to maintain, to gain control, *little* may be accomplished.   486-1

Incoordination of the nervous system in a 40-year-old woman. Note here that hypnosis is also recommended for a second problem: It is proposed as part of a broader treatment regimen related to the overcoming of certain allergies.

Now, as we find, the allergies in this body have reached such states and conditions as to form the pathological and psychological reactions. And, to be of any great material aid in correcting these conditions, there will need to be those preparations of the body, with the chemical changes prepared for the body, and then the use of the psychological reactions to create those coordinations between the sympathetic and the cerebrospinal nervous systems. . .

Q-1. What causes the tingling in the sole of my left foot all the time?

A-1. Because of the connections along the nerve centers, and these will be parts of the suggestions made under the hypnosis; that there will be the perfect coordination through the centers of the body—between sympathetic and cerebrospinal system. This is particularly indicated in the sacral and lumbar area nerves.

Q-2. What causes the neuritis in my left side whenever I put on a pair of shoes, or brassiere, or glasses with plastic frames? How can I get over it?

A-2. These, as indicated, are allergies through the sympathetic system, and are to be overcome through the suggestive treatments, following the light treatments as indicated, and through the same period the taking of the properties to change the chemical reactions in the body.   3125-1

Arthritis in a 26-year-old woman. In this case hypnosis is recommended as an aid to self-study, i.e., the mental portion of a holistic treatment program that also includes particular physical procedures.

Q-1. If treatments are carefully followed, is it indicated how long it will be before a condition of normalcy is reached?

A-1. This will depend upon the attitude of the individual entity. As indicated, the psychological condition must be approached through the mental self. Begin with the study of self, which may be best done by suggestive forces to the body through hypnosis.

3483-1

Behavioral and motivational problems in a teenager. In this case we probably should not interpret some of the details of Cayce's answer to be generally applicable (i.e., the number of treatments, the length of time for each treatment, etc.). However, in this passage the source of the Cayce readings clearly endorses the therapeutic possibilities of hypnosis. Take special note, in the discourse section preceding the questions, of the strong emphasis placed on the awakening of the personal will and the way in which hypnosis is seen only in the light of helping that awakening.

Then, it is of the mental-emotional body that these conditions are being met, as it were, under a karmic influence in the present.

Since much has *been* accomplished in the physical coordination in the body, we find that these conditions may be the more materially aided in the present by inhibiting the mental forces through psychopathic or hypnotic impressions—to arouse the *mental forces* to the natural resistances in the body.

For, as we find, while these conditions are under such a period that these may make for the greater activity in these directions, this—as we would find—would bring the better reactions *now,* or under the present conditions.

xvii

This should be done by those, then, who may *enable* the body to give the greater expression of its *own will* influence upon the activities of the coordinating forces between the sympathetic and cerebrospinal *impulse* reflection in the vocal activities of the body.

As we find, it would only require some eight to ten such treatments to induce the body—so long as it is in the *physical* health as in the present—to overcome the condition.

Ready for questions.

Q-1. Can the hypnotic suggestions be given by those in charge now?

A-1. This, as we find, may be superimposed by the spiritual reactions, but there is needed as much of the *mental* and *physical* reaction as the spiritual *import* upon the body.

If such suggestions were made continuously as the body loses itself in sleep, it would require somewhat a longer manner or way; but may be done by those in charge.

Q-2. What hypnotist would you suggest as being the correct one to give the treatments to this body?

A-2. As we find, such an one as Taylor—Chas. Taylor, New York—54th St.—57th—54 St., as we find, is the address; or Daniel or such as that.

Q-3. If the decision is for those in charge to give the suggestions, just what suggestion should be given?

A-3. That there would be, through the very vital forces of self, the raising of that vibration necessary for making coordinations in the activities of the responses in speech; *through* the powers of the spiritual activity in the body, in *HIS* name!

Q-4. If the hypnotist is decided on, how often should the treatments be given, and how long?

A-4. About every day for the first three or four days; then it may be every other day for the rest of the time. Ten to twelve such treatments should eliminate the greater cause of the conditions.

Q-5. How long should the body be kept in the hypnotic state for treatment?

A-5. From an hour to two hours.

Q-6. Would the hypnotist be able to arouse the will to speak?

A-6. To overcome that inhibition that is caused by the motivative activity in the impulsive forces of the body itself; yes.

Q-7. What should be the suggestion to be given by the hypnotist?

A-7. This is to be very powerful and strong. Various ones use different formulas.

Q-8. Any other suggestions for the body at this time?

A-8. We would keep the spiritual imports in the activities of the body, to make for a balancing in the mental and the physical activities. 146-10

Behavior problem in a child. In this case the behavior difficulty is hand-wringing, but we find similar treatment procedures recommended in other readings for problem children. Take note that the time period for the hypnosis session is "to the body as it sleeps"—although, to be consistent with the way this procedure is presented in other readings for children, it most likely means in that state as the body is *falling asleep.* The recommended helper—or hypnotist, in this instance—is to be someone highly sympathetic to the child's needs, such as a parent.

Q-3. Is there anything we can do to get her to stop wringing her hands?

A-3. Only applying those things that will alter the present nervous reactions in the system will change same. *This* body, would be well for the suggestions to be made under the influence of hypnosis, or autosuggestion to the body as it sleeps. This must be made by someone in sympathy with the activities of the body, and *this* would relieve such stress on the general system. 2253-3

Epilepsy in a 34-year-old woman and a 31-year-old man. In the first example below, autosuggestion or autohypnosis (i.e., self-hypnosis) is clearly recommended as a procedure for changing certain habitual mental attitudes which might otherwise block a healing. In the second instance, hypnosis was encouraged as a tool whereby post-hypnotic suggestion could help to stabilize the beneficial changes previously effected by osteopathic manipulations.

> We find that a great deal better condition may be brought for this body if there is the ability of the mental attitudes to be so changed as to allow same. And as we find, autosuggestion would be the manner through which this might be the better accomplished; combined with the applications for the physical disturbances, which we will give.   1699-1

> Then, after the tenth treatment or tenth week have the correction by suggestion in subjugating the conscious mind, so that the reactions will be sustained by the post suggestions in such a state to the body that the response may be the greater to the manipulations osteopathically given from then on.   3133-1

A troublesome past-life memory in a 28-year-old man. In this case the reading describes past-life influences which have led to a psychological tendency to "get even" with others as well as an impulse to show off power. Hypnosis is suggested as a procedure for healing this condition. We might well expect that other attitudinal and emotional patterns which have an origin in the recent or distant past might be transformed in a similar fashion through hypnosis.

> And there should be applied, in a psychological manner, that which would aid the inner self in putting aside this determination to "get even" with others; as well as that feeling of the needs for the expression to show the power of the personality.

> This as we find would be best accomplished by subjugating the physical consciousness and using the inner or soul consciousness to describe conditions that

are to be eliminated from the consciousness; by hypnosis.   1978-1

The above excerpts demonstrate an impressive variety of ailments and difficulties for which the Cayce readings at least at some time recommended hypnosis. There are other case histories, however, in which hypnosis was discouraged. Any honest and systematic study of this topic should look at these instances with equal care.

Loss of voice in a 31-year-old woman. Ironically, as a young man, Edgar Cayce himself received help through hypnosis for this same difficulty. However, for the individual receiving this reading, hypnosis is mentioned only as a last resort. Other physical procedures are described and the recipient of the reading is encouraged to work with these other treatment modalities first.

One is the subjugation of the body's consciousness by one that may overpower the mental body by suggestions to the psychic forces. But this we would *not* suggest, save as a last resort.   2696-1

Behavior problems in a teenager. This case is mentioned not so much because hypnosis is directly discouraged, but because it includes a particular kind of caution. This same type of caution is found in a number of cases. The concern here is that the *hypnotist* be very carefully selected. Implicit in the response to the question is the recommendation that hypnosis be employed only if a trusted and high-idealed individual can be located to administer the hypnotic induction. The second excerpt from another case makes the same point in an even more direct fashion. Of course, the need to choose an outside hypnotist is automatically eliminated when people make *their own* self-hypnosis tapes.

Q-13. Could hypnotism be used in his case?

A-13. It might be used, but be *mindful* of who would use same!   146-3

It is also dangerous to submit to submerging of self through hypnosis, unless the body-mind of such an operator is in accord with *constructive* forces in a body!
458-1

Epilepsy in a 21-year-old woman. Whereas we saw previous instances in which hypnotherapy was recommended for epilepsy, in another case it is discouraged. This apparent contradiction stresses an important point about the way in which we attempt to draw conclusions from our study of the Cayce readings given for a variety of people. Particularly in the case of the health readings, recommendations are often quite specialized. The overall condition for which Cayce attempts to diagnose and prescribe treatment procedures is not just a set of physical symptoms; it also includes the psychological and spiritual state as well. Even for two people with the same physical, symptomatic difficulties, quite different conditions might exist in the mind or soul. To the extent that Cayce was successful in reading the individual holistically, it makes sense that differences in treatment procedures may emerge for the same disease in different people. For whatever reason, this individual was told that hypnotherapy would not be appropriate at this time in her life for this particular ailment.

Q-2. Would hypnotic influence be applied to body through materia medica or through hypnotherapy?

A-2. Through materia medica, for that as may come through the imaginative system—or hypnotherapy, or hypnotic influence—is too dangerous in conditions of this nature.   543-3

Despite these cases in which individuals were cautioned against the use of hypnosis or in which they were warned to be very careful, there are enough cases in which hypnosis is strongly recommended to indicate that we can conclude that this therapeutic procedure is worthy of our study. Since this book by Henry Bolduc focuses principally on self-hypnosis, the caution we find in the Edgar Cayce readings about carefully selecting a hypnotist is not as significant (except the care we must take in doing the best possible job for ourselves in using autosuggestion). Overall, there seems to be in the Cayce readings general support for the use of suggestive therapeutics in changing troublesome habit patterns. So we might conclude that the suggestion cycles in this book which deal with habits would be quite consistent with the philosophy of the readings.

Since the readings also frequently mention hypnosis as an adjunct to other physical and medicinal treatment procedures, we might conclude that self-hypnosis can often be a useful addition to treatment procedures which one is already employing under the direction of a physician. In the case of a very severe physical or psychological problem, however, prayer, meditation, and dreams might be used in a decision-making procedure for guidance in reaching a personal choice about the appropriateness of self-hypnosis for one of these more severe problems. (That step-by-step inner guidance procedure is described in a number of A.R.E. Press publications, such as *Understand and Develop Your ESP.*)

The very way in which the Cayce readings describe what happens in hypnosis provides us with helpful insights about its proper use. The readings speak of the hypnotic state as a genuine altered state of consciousness in which we experience the quieting or subjugation of the "normal mind" of the body, sometimes referred to as the personality. The purpose of these subjugations of the personality mind is to allow a deeper and stronger mind to become more influential. In some cases the readings refer to this stronger mind as the "soul-mind," "inner self" or "individuality." The problem that we so often face is that the normal mind or personality mind fights against the very conditions that might otherwise effect a change or a healing. Through hypnosis it is possible to make that mental state temporarily more passive (i.e., less controlling) and allow a deeper level of mind to assert its influence.

As we see in the first excerpt below (given for a 50-year-old woman with "sleeping sickness" or narcolepsy), hypnosis can be seen as a process whereby the strong, purposeful conscious mind of the hypnotist temporarily plays the role of the patient's own soul-mind in giving suggestions for change. We can well see why it is crucial to choose a hypnotist in whom one feels an affinity of ideal and life direction. As the hypnotist's work progresses, it should not make the patient increasingly dependent upon his or her exterior influence, but rather serve to awaken the inner will and wisdom of the patient's own soul-mind. Look carefully at these two excerpts in which the inner workings of hypnosis are described.

> Now the repression or action over these can only be removed by an active mind taking of the soul-mind over this body, through the suppression of the normal mind of this body by that of a stronger mind—or an equal mind—to remove from this condition, so that the thought or the action given to the nerve force, to make the proper vibration in the body at this time, will receive its active principle from that of another mind than this one.

> In other words, put the body under what is commonly called hypnotic influence to bring about the normal condition of the action of the body itself. This can be done. Then we will find that the body will be brought to a normal state. It will go through some three to four months of treatment, if followed as we have given here, yet it can return to itself if the body is allowed to think on these things.   4506-1

> Hence the subjugation through those of a subliminal nature, to reach that inner self through the suggestion, see? As suggestion is to the mind, the builder, then we will find, by the subjugation of the own personnel [personal], or personality, in the present condition, we would bring that, through proper suggestion, which would build in a normal manner. . .Some 6 to 10 such subjugations [hypnosis—suggestive therapy] should be sufficient, were these properly given. . .for, as we find at present, when suggestions are given for the physical benefit, these the body fights against. This must be broken down through subjugation of the subliminal, or the inner self. Suggestion lending that control, the personality, while in suggestion, acts to that of building from within—the mental building, see?
>   186-2

The ideas in these two readings are especially instructive, considering the task to which Henry Bolduc invites you in this book. Following his encouragement to work with self-hypnosis and make your own autosuggestion tape recordings, you act as your own hypnotist. As you work with these suggested wordings for self-hypnosis cycles, put yourself in a special frame of mind while you make your tape recordings for later use. Become your own inner self. Become that deeper soul-mind with its high ideals, strength of will, and commitment to growth, change, and healing. Then as you use these recordings, you can claim the best of what the Edgar Cayce readings promised is available to us as a tool for transformation and growth through hypnotic mind-building techniques.

Mark Thurston, Ph.D.
Director
Educational Development Division
   of A.R.E.

CHAPTER ONE

The Inner Mind

"...as [a man] thinketh in his heart, so is he..."
Proverbs 23:7

People could not believe it! A school bus loaded with 26 children had just disappeared. The children had left their homes as usual that morning, but neither they nor the bus had ever arrived at school.

For many agonizing days in Chowchilla, California, there were no clues to this mystery. Then, as suddenly as they had vanished, they were found, along with the bus, less than 100 miles from home. The children and driver were safe, but when police questioned them for facts, they could not recall what had happened to them.

The victims all knew they had been kidnaped, but due to stress they couldn't remember any details. Even the F.B.I. had little success in helping their recall. Everyone seemed too confused and possibly afraid to remember.

As a last resort, the police asked Dr. William Kroger, a professional hypnotist, to use hypnosis to help unlock the victims' painful unconscious memories of the event. In his fear-filled conscious state, the bus driver, Frank Ray, told him that he remembered nothing. But after Dr. Kroger directed the use of hypnotic time regression techniques, the driver was able after 20 minutes to recall valuable information that led police to the kidnapers.

Ray recalled how the kidnapers had seized and buried the bus, trapping him and the 26 children six feet underground in a gravel quarry. "We were scared out of our minds," he admitted. Using their bare hands and combs, pencils and spoons, the driver and children eventually tunneled their way through the six feet of earth. Under hypnosis, Ray clearly recalled details of the episode. He described the kidnapers' white van and gave all but one of the numbers on the license plates. With this information, the police were able to apprehend the kidnapers and the case was closed.

Hypnosis, a valuable tool in police work, can help people remember details clearly. In the first seven years of using hypnosis as an investigative tool, the Los Angeles Police Department has had significant results in over 600 interviews. Police departments in other cities are training their own staffs in the use of hypnosis, while some have hypnotists on call. Across the country more than 1,000 detectives have been taught to use this technique for gaining important information. Some witnesses, however, have given incorrect information while under hypnosis and others have even lied—demonstrating that under hypnosis people always have free will and can make mistakes. The human mind is not perfected yet, and using hypnosis to help solve crimes is fairly new and highly experimental. However, there are other time-tested areas for applying hypnosis that have proven successful. These applications have been developing for years and are becoming more and more widespread.

Giant steps have been taken in the health field since 1958 when the Council on Mental Health of the American Medical Association approved the use of hypnosis by trained physicians. Hypnosis is now commonly used as an anesthetic in childbirth and dentistry. Medical science knows that hypnotic subjects can be taught to control such involuntary functions as pulse rate and blood pressure. Hypnosis is being used experimentally for eliminating warts and in controlling cancer. As more of the mind's potential is explored, hypnosis emerges as a valuable new tool for mankind.

Sports is another innovative field for hypnosis. Sports teams use a "mood room" equipped with hypnotherapeutic tapes to increase players' self-confidence and enthusiasm. Both professional and Olympic class athletes use hypnosis techniques to attain better concentration and stamina. Many creative people, such as writers, artists, musicians, dancers, and movie stars, credit hypnosis with having helped their careers.

One of the most common uses for hypnosis today is in controlling habits. Weight reduction and cigarette elimination are common goals, but any habit can be changed and a positive life style developed. Other important areas are improving health, strengthening memory, managing stress, conquering fears, developing a sense of humor, attracting abundance, instilling motivation, and preparing for personal changes. These and other important topics are covered later in this book.

Hypnosis has been used in uncommon ways also. Edgar Cayce, the famous psychic of Virginia Beach, would enter a self-hypnotic state in which he was able to diagnose illnesses and give physical, mental and spiritual guidance that helped many people, most of whom he never met. He needed to be given only the name and address of a patient and would tune in telepathically to the individual's mind and body as easily as if he were in the same room with the person. He needed no other information regarding the patient.

When Edgar Cayce died in 1945, he left documented stenographic records of the telepathic-clairvoyant statements he had given for more than 6,000 different people over a period of 43 years. The Association for Research and Enlightenment, Inc., a psychical research society, was formed in 1931 to preserve and research this data. Its library in Virginia Beach is open to the public and contains copies of 14,256 of Edgar Cayce's psychic readings.

Thomas Sugrue, Cayce's biographer, writes in *There Is a River* that the story of Edgar Cayce properly belongs in the history of hypnosis. In numerous readings the "sleeping" Cayce (he *looked* asleep while in the trance state) recommended hypnosis or suggestive therapeutics as a method of help and benefit for people. In some readings he said *not* to use hypnosis or suggestion. Perhaps it was because in Cayce's time there probably were very few (if any) established hypnosis centers or clinics, no self-help cassette tapes, and many hypnotists of that time were merely stage entertainers.

So what exactly is this technique called *hypnosis*? How is it used to help solve crimes, improve sports performance, help someone become slimmer, and aid psychic ability, among other things?

The word "hypnosis" stems from *hypnos*, the Greek word for sleep. However, people experiencing hypnosis are not actually sleeping—far from it! They may *appear* to others to be asleep, but they can think, talk, open their eyes, respond to suggestion, and move in any way. People experiencing hypnosis are usually aware of their surroundings and can hear other sounds besides the voice of the hypnotist.

Hypnosis, like love, is difficult to define because every person experiences it a little differently. The hardest part most people have with it is simply getting past the word "hypnosis."

Hypnosis is a tool for modern minds; it is 100% natural. Sometimes it is called a *waking* dream, at other times a *working* dream. It means different things to different people (even the experts can't agree on how to define it!). Although many have been helped and inspired by hypnosis, some think of it as only a stage show; the reality, however, is somewhere in between. Far more profound than a mere show, there is nothing really amazing about hypnosis except the use of the unlimited potential of the human mind.

It is also a method of relaxing the physical body and utilizing another level of awareness through suggestion and visualization. This level of awareness, called "alpha," refers to a state of electrical activity in the brain. We all experience this activity as we go into regular nighttime sleep and again later as we awaken in the morning.

The levels of hypnosis are measured by brain-wave frequency. Technically, sleep researchers, biofeedback* technicians, and medical practitioners look upon the human brain as consisting of four levels of activity, each having a particular cycle-per-second rate.

Although there is still ambiguity in this new field, researchers have called the normal, everyday waking state *beta. Alpha* is that transitional time people experience when they are half awake and half asleep. *Theta* occurs in deep hypnosis, intense meditation, and during the early stages of nighttime sleep. *Delta,* perhaps the least understood level of the human mind, is the deepest sleep or unconsciousness.

Most people experience the hypnotic state when they are in alpha, where attention is focused on their objective but where they may be aware of noises or of other people in the room. They usually have recollection of most of the session unless a specific suggestion is otherwise given and accepted. Because it is such a familiar feeling (people experience it at least twice a day and oftentimes also when watching television or even daydreaming), some people, after their first session, question whether they were truly hypnotized. This altered state of consciousness is called "trance" by some people and "controlled relaxation" by others.

---

*Biofeedback uses instrumentation to monitor the nonconscious changes in biological information, such as blood pressure, muscle tension, and brain-wave activity which may lead to the control of involuntary functions. It then makes information about these physical processes available to the practitioner, allowing him or her to attain voluntary control of internal states.

The state of hypnosis is intriguing, often ambiguous. The old-fashioned, silent-movie devotee may probably insist that it is magic, yet others may imagine it to be the scary stereotype as demonstrated in some old movies. Some think it an impossibility or a fraud, convinced there must be a trick to it. To a night-club audience it is entertaining and amusing. A growing number of people realize that hypnosis is a key that can unlock dormant parts of the human mind and produce results far more enduring than night-club stunts.

Despite the misconceptions, hypnosis is not really mysterious. Once learned, it is a *tool* which allows a person to use more of his or her mind and to use it more dynamically and effectively. Hypnosis is relaxed receptivity with increased perception, a state of deep relaxation which quiets the body and opens the mind. With its defenses down, the mind is especially open to suggestion, the type of which is determined by a person's goals and ideals—the reasons for wanting to use hypnosis.

Like a gardener, you choose the specific thought-seeds you want to plant. Hypnosis helps you to care for and nourish those thought-seeds to grow and bear fruit. Your subconscious mind is your secret garden where the thoughts you plant grow to become your reality. This garden is far more fertile than you may realize, so plan carefully! As the Edgar Cayce readings often assert, "Thoughts are things."

This book will suggest to you how to plant thoughts by making your own self-hypnosis cassette tape, and how to take more control of your own mind and gear it to the accomplishment of your objectives. Self-help tapes are tools to build your mind and remodel your life the way *you* want it to be. They are an idea whose time has come. They will help you develop mental strength and put the "self" back into self-help. You alone use your free will and choose what you are going to plant—and reap—in your mind.

Here is an example of how this process works. Suppose Joe has been biting his fingernails for as long as he can remember. Over the years, Joe's subconscious mind received a little signal click whenever his teeth bit down on a nail. Click after click, for years on end, Joe's habit signaled his subconscious that this was what he wanted to do. But then one day he decides to stop nail-biting. Joe grits his teeth, musters up all his reserves of willpower, and buries his hands in his pockets. But somehow Joe's fingers find their way into his mouth again.

What's the problem? Until they are reprogramed, Joe's mind and body will continue to react to all those little clicks his subconscious mind has programed into his conscious mind over the years. So it is still sending impulses out to his hands as though he had nothing to say or do about it. Now Joe wants to change course, but his inner mind continues along the same rut because it is conforming to the old programing. In time, its own sweet time, his mind may get the message. But does he want to wait that long?

To change a habit that has taken root in the subconscious, Joe first needs to reach and communicate with his subconscious—his inner mind—and plant new information. Working solely at the conscious level to get rid of a habit is like trying to weed a lawn of dandelions by skimming off the tops. The roots remain intact, locked in the earth, and before one knows it, the weed is sprouting again. Hypnosis cultivates the inner mind where all the roots are intertwined and now Joe painlessly extracts them session by session, planting something better in their place. Soon the torn fingernails heal, and Joe is proud of his success and accomplishment.

You can hack at the dandelions in your life, or you can use your mind to get to the root of the matter. Using the principles and procedures in this book, you can also achieve success, but it is important to realize that your success—or lack of it—is yours. It is you, the person making the self-help tape, who chooses to accomplish a goal and does what's necessary to achieve it. Meaningful communication with your subconscious requires your full consent and cooperation. Hypnosis can't make you do anything that you do not choose to do—but it can help you get more out of living.

A *hypnotist* is the individual who guides another into the alpha state by using a variety of techniques to help the subject bypass his or her conscious, analytical outer mind in order to reach the subconscious, intuitive inner mind. This is similar to a person taking a bypass on a freeway, thus avoiding a crowded city, in order to reach a destination more quickly. The human mind works on two levels: the outer conscious level and the inner subconscious level. You can understand this by visualizing the planet Earth. The conscious mind can be likened to the solid land masses, while the subconscious to the fathomless oceans. These two parts of the mind can function separately or in harmony. Hypnosis is a refined form of communication that harmonizes your conscious and subconscious minds.

The Edgar Cayce readings define mind as "That which is the active force in an animate object; that is the spark, or image of the Maker. . .*Mind* is *that* that reasons the impressions from the senses, as they manifest before the individual. *The active principle that governs man."* (3744-1)

The readings speak of the subconscious mind as "That lying between the soul and spirit forces within the entity, and is reached more thoroughly when the conscious mind is under subjugation of the soul forces of the individual or physical body. We may see manifestation in those of the so-called spiritual-minded people. The manifestation of the subconscious in their action. That portion of the body, better known as the one that propagates or takes care of the body—physical, mental, moral or whatnot, when it is not able to take care of itself. *Subconscious* is the *un*conscious force." (3744-1)

On an unconscious level, your brain regulates heartbeat, body temperature, and breathing in response to any physical activity you undertake. Your subconscious mind, being aware of this, always protects you. It never goes to sleep and at night it takes full control. When you begin to drift off to sleep, your conscious mind ceases functioning. For many people this twilight time between wakefulness and sleep is the birthplace of creative ideas, some of which might have been forming in their minds for weeks and then suddenly surface when they least expect it.

There are no boundaries that your subconscious cannot cross. It is like a dutiful soldier—it does what it's told; it only reacts. Yet it is the conscious mind that acts and makes decisions. The Cayce readings explain it this way: "The *conscious* means *that* that is able to be manifested in the physical plane through one of the senses." (3744-1) You need to desire something consciously before you can instruct your subconscious to achieve it. Problems arise only when these two selves are not in harmony—when what you think you want is not what you really want. Meditating on your goals and ideals is one way to reconcile the difference.

Recent brain and mind research reveals differences between the right and left halves of the brain. The left side is logical and rational; the right side is intuitive and visual. The self-hypnosis programs or "cycles" in this book are a full-brain experience, using both practical suggestions and creative visualizations.

The human mind has a creative factor and a critical factor, both of which are necessary for a healthy, productive life. The *creative factor* can take you anywhere; it is the child of your subconscious mind. It is as unquestioning as a computer which complies with whatever information is programed into it. Tell a computer that the world is flat, and it will "believe" it because it does not know any better. Yet this very naiveté can be a dynamic tool, because the creative factor of your mind truly believes you can do anything.

In the alpha-hypnotic state, you can apply the creative factor to bypass negative conditioning and reprogram your mind to respond as you wish. Whether you want to change a habit or reconstruct your attitudes, your creative factor's message is "I can; I will; I know that I can make it happen." The creative factor frees your unlimited potential, like the sails of a ship that propel you ahead.

The *critical factor,* a feature of your conscious mind, is more like the rudder of a ship: It can keep you on course and is the pilot of all your inhibitions. It sends such signals as "I can't; I won't"; or, "I haven't been able to before, so I can't now." Its influence is necessary when it reminds you, for example, of the folly of feeding crocodiles by hand. But it needs to be overcome when it paralyzes you into crystallized habit patterns, when healthy caution becomes crippling fear. Ideally, your critical factor screens impulses, filters out what is harmful, and helps you set realistic goals.

Balance is the goal between your practical, critical mind and the abundant flow of your creative mind. There is a middle ground, an equilibrium, between the weight of an anchor and casting all caution to the wind.

An overworked critical factor and negative conditioning are both anchors that are difficult to hoist alone. With time and enough pulling, the anchor might be lifted, but chances are (like the roots of an old habit) you'll find the anchor dragging the bottom or wedged in a crevice somewhere deep in your mind. Raising it with help and with the proper tools will get you sailing onward to your destination.

Do you think you'll never learn how to sail your ship? Then you probably never will. Few people have accomplished anything that they thought was impossible. But wait a minute! Stop and think. Who says you can't sail around the world or hike on the Great Wall of China? How did you come by all that self-doubt in the first place? Your self-image, who you think you are, is influenced by your attitudes and the attitudes of the people around you. All too often you may think a goal is unreachable only because you have been told over and over, in many different ways, that it is impossible. This kind of thinking is the stuff of which anchors are made. Anchors do have their place, but they can be a hindrance when you want to start going and growing.

Hypnosis may not perform miracles overnight, but it can help heave anchors. Reprograming your mind with a self-hypnosis tape can help you control or eliminate habits, create a positive new identity for yourself, and develop latent talents and abilities. The process for this is called a "cycle" or a "program." A *cycle* is a personal program for positive change.

In the field of computers, a program is an organized group of instructions to tell the computer what to do. It must be in a language that the machine can understand. Similarly, in the area of the mind, a program is an organized group of verbal and visual instructions to tell the subconscious what to do. It, too, must be in clear and simple language that the mind understands.

The word "cycle" describes the complete hypnosis program, including both specific suggestions and constructive imagination exercises. A cycle is defined by *Webster's* as: "A period of time during which something becomes established." Cycle is also defined as a full turnabout, a well-rounding and a full change.

The cycles in this book can bring new cycles of success into your life. For example, using a self-confidence cycle, you can build a more assertive personality and become a dynamo of accomplishment after a lifetime of floundering. Although the transformation often seems miraculous, the real miracle-workers are your ideals, sincere desire, proper suggestion, and creative imagination. By using positive suggestions and continually picturing yourself as self-confident, you feed new positive programing into your inner mind. The idea is nothing new. It is as old as the book of Proverbs in the Bible.

By teaching you to tap into the energy of your creative imagination, hypnosis opens up a panorama of exciting possibilities. Imagination is the cornerstone of reality. From the invention of the wheel to the launching of satellites in outer space, every great idea and invention began in someone's imagination. Belief—in yourself and in what you can achieve—is all you need to start turning your dreams into reality.

Soon you will see what self-hypnosis cycles can do for you in using the vast potential of your mind to reshape your reality. You can develop your memory, creativity, and public-speaking ability. You can transform nervousness into helpful, productive energy. Fears can be reduced or eliminated and a positive self-image cultivated. You can remember where you misplaced an object or ease yourself to sleep more easily at night. You can prepare for surgery or the birth of a child. You can attract more love and find greater fulfillment in life. You can develop your psychic ability and become a dynamic part of the human adventure. In making self-hypnosis tapes, there is almost no limit to what you can do.

Now, before you say that all this sounds impossible, pause for a moment and consider that we live in a time when the impossible has become commonplace. In the brief span of decades we have taken giant steps—from Kitty Hawk to the moon! Yet, there was a time when man, thinking that he couldn't fly, did not. Today we can even fly in solar-powered aircraft. Your mind is your most valuable resource. Your future is in your mind today. Opening the mind can lead to undreamed-of futures, endless avenues of exploration, and scientific self-improvement.

CHAPTER TWO
Dynamic Change

Within every person lies a desire to step out of the past, to strive beyond the present, and to reach out toward tomorrow. Dynamic change is active and potent, setting a new direction that is full of force and energy. It is far more than breaking out of ingrained habit patterns; it is building a better future.

"Rut-busting" is a word that vividly describes this change and growth process—the act of freeing yourself from stifling patterns, negative addictions, and unwanted habits. "Busting out" of old ruts is breaking away or rising above what you may perceive as a dead past or a futile present. This can happen on a physical, mental, emotional, or spiritual level—or it can happen on all these levels at the same time.

Helen Keller, who experienced many dynamic changes in her life, said, "Life is either a daring adventure or nothing at all." But change and growth have their fearful moments. Eric Hoffer in *The Ordeal of Change* (Harper & Row, 1963) wrote, "It is my impression that no one really likes the new. We are afraid of it. It is not only as Dostoevski put it that 'taking a new step, uttering a new word is what people fear most.' Even in slight things the experience of the new is rarely without some stirring of foreboding."

13

If you are ready for change, you may find a lever to pry yourself out of an old rut. According to the laws of physics, a lever needs a fulcrum or pivotal point in order in to work. The fulcrum is the point of change. Following the "laws of life," change can be triggered by choice or by a crisis. A crisis is defined as a decisive point or condition —a turning point. Your self-hypnosis cassette tape will be your fulcrum or point of change where you will gain more leverage in your life. In other words, *you choose how you want to change.*

Here is an example of how a crisis becomes a method for drastic change. A few years ago a woman went to her minister for counseling. She was concerned and upset about her younger brother who was having marital problems. In his desperate confusion he had turned to alcohol and drugs, and even lost his job. The sister hoped the minister would help "straighten him out." In his wisdom, the minister said that the brother himself would first have to ask for help. He realized that all too often people want to change others. He predicted that her brother would most likely experience a crisis point which would demand major changes in his life—and that it was important that the changes be of his own choice. Years of practical experience had taught the minister that sometimes individuals have to go to the very bottom before they ask for help and start again on their way back up.

As difficult as it was for this woman to accept her minister's advice, the years proved his logic and intuition to be correct. The younger brother's life surely did hit rock bottom. One day his wife simply walked out. But now, with the perspective of time, he feels her leaving was the turning-point in his self-destructive plunge. Eventually both the wife and the husband began to re-evaluate their lives and to decide on a practical plan of action. Time, patience, family counseling, and therapy allowed them to understand and accept themselves better and to make needed and positive changes.

Times of change seem to be crisis periods because of people's fear of them, and they are often resisted "tooth and nail." You may tenaciously clutch and hold to the status quo—that which you are used to—and think you want the comfort and security of old habits even though you have outgrown your need for them. But eventually these outgrown habits may start to pinch.

This pinched feeling lets you know that there is a turning-point taking place in your life, and then—all of a sudden—you may feel the pain of a full-blown crisis. Contrary to what it may seem, this is a positive and very important time, for you can turn during this period to your inner self—that small voice within—for guidance. You can re-evaluate your life with prayer and meditation, then begin changing it with self-hypnotic positive programing. *Now* is the time that things can get done. This is your turning-point for change, growth, accomplishment, and self-transformation—the birth of a new you.

To the human fetus, safe in the mother's womb, the day of birth is a day of crisis. This is "rut-busting" at its earliest! Yet, if that special and important day were not chosen—or forced—who would ever be born? It seems that one needs change almost as much as one needs oxygen. Change is growth; and growing is a lifetime endeavor, as learning does not end with high school or college. You learn to create your tomorrow by changing first your thoughts and then your actions.

If what you are now doing isn't working the way you desire, then choose to do things differently. If the way you are going isn't giving you positive results, then go a different way. You can begin dynamic change by doing something you haven't done before. When you come to the crossroads, you can choose new directions. You can set different goals, make different decisions, get a different job, or find different friends. You can change the way you do things; you can specifically form new patterns in a thoughtful, realistic way.

Since each person is unique, no set formula for making changes is suggested. However, a few examples are given below to hint at the possibilities.

Charles, who recently graduated from high school, lacked any real direction in his life. Hopelessly unsure about the future, he decided to camp out alone for a week by a sheltered lake in the cool, green woods of New England. Seeking insight into his soul's purpose, he was determined to find real direction. Charles examined his ideals, established a practical, realistic goal, and subsequently fulfilled it. The dynamic change in his life was that week of seclusion, introspection, and intimacy with his own mind.

Deborah had a major weight problem. Not knowing anything about self-hypnosis, she had tried all sorts of diets—to no avail. An opportunity came to house-sit at a remote mansion filled with valuable antiques. "What a great job," she said. "I will earn money, be alone to read and study, and I'll bring no food along except fruit and vegetables." It seemed a drastic step but "cold turkey" (not cold turkey sandwiches!), applied to a dynamic change situation, worked well for Deborah. Through this unusual approach she gained better health and financial reward.

Carmen was reared in a negative and repressive environment that caused her to be shy, withdrawn, and introverted. When she grew up, she made a careful choice to live in a small informal group home. Through the daily give-and-take, social interaction with more positive people, and the caring family atmosphere, Carmen quickly overcame her shyness. Putting herself in a better environment was a dynamic step in human relations, in understanding and in acceptance. Today Carmen is more confident, assured, and is considered a "style-setter."

Patrick always had a yen for travel, but with a dead-end job he never had enough money. One day, after reading a book by Henry David Thoreau, he packed his clothes and a sleeping bag and started his quest for personal discovery and new horizons. Today Pat is an experienced world traveler, speaks several languages, and has become the author of a travel and guide book.

These examples illustrate what creating a change did for others. Now you can "create" opportunities for yourself. "Knock, and it shall be opened. . ." (Matthew 7:7) Sometimes an opportunity enters quietly, all on its own, or it may come barging in unannounced and uninvited. When you study any crisis objectively, you may obtain insight into how it can be a springboard to new life and opportunity.

For some people, dynamic change—breaking free—is truly a major accomplishment. It is a full remodeling, a complete process, a new life. For others, it might be nothing more complicated than erasing an old habit and creating a positive one instead. For some, success is achieved through a series of small, quiet acts; for others, a single courageous, heroic stand. If you want to accomplish just a little, then do just a little. If you want to achieve a lot, then do a lot.

Edgar Cayce once explained it this way: "Be reasonable with self; be reasonable with that which is being attempted to be done! Consider this: Compare self, as it were (and it is in very much the same condition), to an automobile that has been stuck in the mud! There would be the rocking back and forth, and the realization that it was going down deeper and deeper and deeper—*but,* if you stopped, or if you went altogether dead, would there be any pulling out? Put more force, more vim, more power within self—and you'll move out!" (911-4)

When you are ready to start moving out—and pulling out—of some of your ruts, here are several questions you can ask yourself:

"Where am I stuck?"

"Which parts of my life feel 'pinched'?"

"Am I in an intellectual, emotional, spiritual, financial, or career rut?"

"What do I want to change and how?"

And the most important question, "How much of my spare time am I willing to invest in a personal recycling, self-help program?"

Whether it's a groove, a rut, or a full-fledged muddy trench you are in, your daily self-hypnosis program can create dynamic change. Twenty-five or thirty minutes of daily programing can significantly improve your life. The real secret, though, involves doing it every day. A modern philosopher said, "Tell me what you do in your spare time and I'll tell you what you'll be a year from now." How true! Your spare time is truly your most valuable time; it is your time for *you.* Apply it well.

All that you achieve will be the direct result of the level of your desire, your time, your thoughts, your purpose, your needs, and your ideals. Only you know what you need or don't need. Like a sculptor, you decide which sharp edges you wish to chisel away and which graceful features you wish to leave intact. Set your own pace and be kind to your mind. You may chisel slowly and methodically, or hammer out big chunks with thundering blows. Work at your best pace and be lovingly definite with yourself.

By making your personal self-hypnosis cassette tape, you help bring about dynamic change. This positive programing enables you to reach your objective by focusing on how you *can* achieve a goal, not why you can't. If you are like most people, you probably have some minor and some major projects on which you would like to start working. The first step is to think about what you want (your goal) and why you want it (your ideal). (In the Cayce readings the ideal is considered as the standard or criterion by which you measure your life.) The hardest part may be deciding what you truly want—and why.

Writing out all your goals (what you want), in the order of importance, will help you to clarify them. Then look within and see why you want them. At first, you may think you want something, only to realize afterward that it may not be in your best interests. You may think, for example, "I want lots of money," yet not have enough discipline or personal responsibility for properly handling "lots" of money. After careful consideration, set out to accomplish your purpose by wisely using your spare time to program for your highest ideals.

With self-hypnosis you can learn to program for almost anything—career, a home, financial security, or a loving relationship. You can also plan for pleasure, entertainment, travel, creative ability, or spiritual development. Goals need not always be business-world oriented or just for people living in the fast lane. (If you are uncertain about which goal or project to start working with, consider the "Preparing for Change" cycle in Chapter Eight.)

It is wise to have specific goals, as your subconscious mind will then actively work toward the accomplishment of them. This process is happening, though, even when your conscious mind is not actively thinking about it. By programing for a goal, however, you have an added edge of ingenuity and determination when opportunities arise.

Setting a goal requires a positive attitude about its eventual completion. Again from the earlier example, people state this very common goal: "I want lots of money." But then they may spend countless hours complaining about their lack of money, their lousy job, their bills, and inflation. All that negative thinking and speaking isn't going to get anybody anything—except maybe more into debt. They are spinning their wheels and getting stuck deeper and deeper in the mud.

A better way to maneuver out of this money rut is to create a positive money consciousness—a financial healing. Think money, but think of it in a pleasant way. Use the "Attracting Abundance Cycle" in Chapter Eight to create a state of mind that attracts money in a constructive way. Money is an energy; it is a means to an end. Invest in *yourself*; remember, money is just metal or paper.

It is *what* money can do for you—how it can help you become a better person—that is important.

One frequently mistaken notion is that having money is the only way to accomplish things. (It's a good way, but not the only way.) Often there are quicker, more direct approaches to achieving goals than through the possession of money. Once you have decided what you truly want and why you want it, then you can program yourself for the actual goal.

Suzanna dreamed of an exciting vacation to an exotic place. She wanted it because she had worked for several years without having a real vacation and needed to get away for a while. She tried to save money for such a trip, but somehow extra cash never seemed to accumulate. After writing down her goal, she tried a new approach. She made this goal known to certain friends who had a positive outlook. Soon she had an offer to go with a family to Hawaii, and helped baby-sit for their children in exchange for the all-expenses-paid trip.

Once you can steer out of the rut, shift your life into passing gear, and start accomplishing your objectives, there are two things to remember. First, be thankful for your continuing success. This is important psychologically. Your mind appreciates the value of a few strokes or a few kind words. Second, avoid returning to an unwanted past. This admonition seems obvious, but it is most important not to backslide. During my years as Director of the Providence (R.I.) Hypnosis Center, I cautioned cigarette-smoking clients not to readdict themselves by playing "I-dare-you-to-try-just-one" games with themselves. Though there was no compulsion or need to smoke after therapy, they were cautioned not to try a cigarette just to see how it tastes. Such games are not only foolish, they are self-defeating and immature.

It is said that change is the one sure thing in life. When we grow as individuals, we are changed in two ways—by circumstance and by choice. We, in turn, change our environment. Change is that which allows our life to move and grow. Life is not static; it ebbs and flows like the tides. Change occurs on individual, local, state, national, and world levels. All life is a constant cycle of birth, death, and rebirth into new forms. The old passes away. The new is born.

World and national changes take many forms. Dynamic changes are happening in such areas as family structures, education, rehabilitation, religion, government, communications, housing, energy sources, food, transportation, and space programs.

The space program, for instance, has captured our interest the past few decades. Untold millions of dollars were spent shooting rockets into outer space with spectacular and important results. Because of economics and a change of consciousness, the search into inner space is now being launched. Mankind is beginning an exciting exploration of the internal self. Inner reality has piqued our interest, with mind becoming the focus of today and the builder of tomorrow, our greatest natural resource.

The year 2000 quickly approaches with its grand expectations. Mind, once the storehouse of secrets, is now revealing its gifts. Best of all, mind exploration and personal development are virtually free. With the small investment of a cassette recorder, you can begin your own mind-building and reprograming exercises. Truly it has been said that the best things in life are free. You only have to seize the opportunity and create your own destiny.

Before you begin designing your personal self-hypnosis program, let's look at the ways that hypnosis *already* has affected your life. "Hidden" hypnosis influences your daily life far more than you may realize.

CHAPTER THREE

Hidden Hypnotist
in Your Life

Whether you are aware of it or not, you live with aspects of hypnosis almost every day of your life. Hypnosis comes packaged in many shapes and sizes that are seldom, if ever, called hypnosis. There is one hypnotist to the right of you and another to your left, but they are not the creaky old stereotypes of the silent movies. They are your friends and relatives, your neighbors, the people you work with, and the person selling products on television.

Hypnosis occurs when your critical factor is persuaded to take a break. With your mental watchdog napping, a choice suggestion or two can easily infiltrate your inner mind. What's more, you don't have to be in a deep trance for a suggestion to take root. You can be watching television, daydreaming, or sunning yourself with friends at the beach. It doesn't matter what you do or where you are; your inner mind responds to chance remarks and subtle suggestions. It is true that planting seeds in your subconscious can be helpful, but weeds can grow there just as well.

For instance, television can be a baby-sitter, entertainer, pacifier, companion, or it can lull your throbbing brain after a hard day. Some people just turn their set on for company when they're alone. Others watch when they are at a loss for anything else to do. Somehow, it always seems to be turned on—and it seems to be everywhere. Therefore, TV is a perfect outlet for advertisers who can reach millions in just a few seconds. There is nothing haphazard about it. The typical advertising agency spends many thousands of dollars mobilizing a small array of specialists and enlisting everyone from psychologists to artists to produce just one television commercial.

A lot of time and money is spent to discover what motivates you, the consumer, to buy a product. One type of specialist goes to work on slogans and jingles, another designs an alluring product package (possibly with subliminal sexual appeal), while still another recruits and rehearses the actors who spearhead the pitch to you.

Great care is given to the image an advertiser wants to convey. When a distinguished, graying executive in a navy pin-stripe suit wants you to subscribe to his favorite financial journal for the sake of your career, a subtle message is being flashed to your subconscious. In pursuit of a different image, another advertiser presents a primly practical young woman (who could be somebody's guidance counselor), explaining the advantages of her down-to-earth panty hose.

The finished commercial gets a few test runs in selected areas, just as a theatrical drama tours Boston and Philadelphia before its Broadway opening. If the commercial passes muster, it is promoted to big-time network television, where it quickly becomes a fixture in your living room and your subconscious.

Commercials are shown more than once. In fact, they are shown unendingly—over and over again; same scene, same actors, same stubborn grease stain, until a kind of mental Novocain™ sets in. During the first few airings, you might actually watch the commercial, but soon you tire of it. You may even try to escape to the bathroom or retreat into your newspaper when it comes on. You think you are paying it no heed.

To your outer mind that commercial is annoying background static. However, the antenna of your inner mind is picking up every word; without your knowledge it is learning things and committing them to memory. Television commercials, like hypnosis, use both visual and verbal suggestions that entice cooperation by dangling a reward in front of you. Consciously, you may not swallow the notion that a new mouthwash will add zip to your love life, but your inner mind sees and hears that programing again and again, even while you think you are not paying attention to it. Once your inner mind accepts an assertion as truth, you react as though it were true.

So the subconscious mind absorbs messages, and, no matter how preposterous or absurd you think the message is, some of it will stick in your mind. Even the ancient Romans realized that no matter how false the message, "something always sticks."

A commercial may suggest that you buy a product for certain reasons. Now logically you may reject the notion. You may even be annoyed by the repetition and the actors. Yet when you are at that section of the grocery store, you may reach unconsciously for that product before any other. Your subconscious mind has received the message and you have responded. The Cayce readings ask, "What would you have your mind-body to become? For that upon which it feeds it becomes, that either by thought, by assimilation, by activity. . ." (262-78)

It is also interesting to hear professional advertisers speak of "hard sell" and "soft sell." Hard sell calls a product by name and is often direct, definite, and somewhat demanding. In hypnotic suggestion this approach is called direct suggestion; it works well with one group of people. Other people respond best to indirect suggestion, which can be likened to soft sell. The soft sell is a subtle and gentle approach; sometimes it uses humor to soothe your defenses. You are never directly told to buy a product; instead, you are shown smiling, happy people using, eating, or drinking the product. This is less direct but often far more potent. Many commercials incorporate both approaches.

Shoppers usually do not buy a product on the basis of information on the label or even the price. They often buy a product because the name is familiar. Or they may identify with its image, having been conditioned by commercials they think they haven't even heard. Advertising agencies, like the hypnotist, have discovered the effectiveness of suggestions delivered at the edge of consciousness. It could be called "purchase by post-hypnotic suggestion." Some viewers believe that the regular daily TV programs have even more hidden messages than the commercials.

There are ways to deal with this constant bombardment of programs and commercials that molds your thoughts with electronic hypnosis. The Cayce readings warn, "For thoughts are things; just as the mind is as concrete as a post or tree or that which has been molded into things of any form." (1581-1) First, get in touch with your inner self and your ideals. Then, increase your awareness of your surroundings and build a more positive personality. Obviously the best solution would be to limit your daily intake of television and other advertising media. Also it would be especially important not to fall asleep with the television on, for then you have almost no defense against commercial input.

The best way to learn about these subtle forms of hypnosis is to study and observe carefully, so that you can recognize and use them to your advantage, as advertisers use them to their advantage. Besides this book's application of self-hypnosis, you can experience other endeavors which utilize intense concentration and a high degree of mental awareness that is reminiscent of the alpha state. Similar experiences, but having separate purposes, include the martial arts, music, dancing, yoga, meditation, and even prayer.

Prayer can be called a form of autosuggestion. Through positive expectation and attitude prayer makes a powerful tool for programing. It is a proven concept that is compelling to the millions who do pray, and the sheer numbers it attracts suggests it works very well.

Prayer is a way of talking with God and can help you attune to your spiritual heritage. There are prayers of thanksgiving and prayers of atonement, but the prayers usually said most fervently are ones of petition. People pray for the things they want, whether peace of mind, a better job, a new car or happiness. Some prayers are idealistic, others materialistic, but all give voice to deeply felt needs. They are as varied as the people who pray.

Though prayers are generally directed heavenward, this approach doesn't stop the inner mind from tuning in. Our conscious and subconscious minds are wedded in the power of belief. Most people, while praying, will separate themselves from their surroundings and become totally absorbed in the words they are speaking to God. Their prayer gives voice to a hope or a need, with the conviction that the hope will be fulfilled or the need met if only the prayer is repeated often and with faith.

Prayer is similar to self-hypnosis in that the person praying turns desires into reality and develops new faith in himself or herself. While self-hypnosis strengthens the subconscious mind, prayer attunes the conscious mind. This is simply stated in the Cayce readings: "...prayer is the *making* of one's conscious self more in attune with the spiritual forces that may manifest in a material world..." (281-13) When you pray, you believe that with God's help all things are possible. You know that God helps those who help themselves, so you work twice as hard to see that your wishes are granted. If seeing is believing, then believing is achieving.

Whether it is conscious as prayer or unconscious as television commercials, there are other forms of hidden hypnosis all around you. Of all the "hidden hypnotists" in your life, your friends, relatives, and neighbors carry the most clout. Their words can cut a path right down to your mental quick—not because they are master mesmerists, but because your defenses are down in their presence. You are usually relaxed around your friends and open to their suggestions, whether good or bad. Because we are all vulnerable in this sense, it is best to choose to be around positive people. You trust your friends, knowing they would never intentionally harm you, but a well-meaning friend who deflates your hopes "for your own good" is abusing your trust.

I encountered a sad example of this sugar-coated sabotage while working with a tremendously obese woman who was in a clinic to lose weight. She had been told again and again by a doting family that they liked her just the way she was. They not only tempted her to overeat ("Come on, Ma, have another one. You know you like to eat!"), but they reinforced her low self-image by telling her that "at her age" it didn't matter how fat she was. The hypnosis center worked with her for one hour a week; but the family had her the rest of the time.

Conditioning by the people around you can often take the form of an unthinking remark or an unconscious gesture. For instance, you might have felt fine until the grocer asked if you had been sick. On the other hand, if someone remarks that you look terrific, how do you feel then? Even a raised eyebrow or the movement of an arm can send signals to your inner mind.

Everywhere people are in constant nonverbal communication with one another through movements called body language, sending and receiving signals without being consciously aware. If you are alert to the innuendo of a posture or gesture, you can find out what the other person really means (which may be very different from the words).

The driver stalled in traffic has reached the boiling point when he rubs the back of his neck. The hand raised to his neck might be an unconscious striking gesture showing that he wants to lash out at the other motorists even though his rational outer mind won't let him do it. Feelings of confidence may be exhibited by the person who steeples his fingers during a conference. Or perhaps he has studied body language and is using it to convince the others that he is in command of the situation.

On an intuitive level, lovers and poker players are particularly adept at reading subliminal signals. Performers, politicians, and salesmen are also skilled body linguists, projecting nonverbal messages that create a subconscious acceptance of what they say. Sometimes what is said is less important than how it is said. You can leave a speech feeling warm toward the speaker, even though you do not remember what was said.

Perhaps, at some point, you feel that you must face too many negative influences. It seems that no matter what you do, where you go or whom you see, someone is waiting to ambush your psyche. But that doesn't mean you must stay home and barricade yourself in a closet. After all, a snare is dangerous only when you don't know it's there. Your knowledge and awareness of the conditioning around you is the best antidote—when you use it. The Cayce readings say, "For it is not altogether true that knowledge is power, but the *application* of knowledge within the self's experience is power." (1908-1)

Use what you are learning and shift your thoughts into positive gear—carefully censor the kind of programing your mind receives. Nurture the seeds and pull the weeds! You can consciously program for the things you want, and learn to intercept the signals your mind gets from the environment and the people around you. Some people make an art of replacing words like "problem" with its positive counterpart "challenge" or "project" or "opportunity" to help budge outmoded attitudes out of their ruts. Edgar Cayce oftentimes advised turning stumbling blocks into stepping-stones.

Positive programing is the surest way to overcome hidden negativity. There is nothing complicated about programing your mind in a constructive way. People do it all the time though they may attach another label to it, like "mind over matter" or as the athlete who "psychs" himself up for a game. Bobby Orr, the former hockey superstar, used to go off by himself before a contest and rehearse the game in his mind. Likewise, your mental imagery and your positive thoughts literally build your future and with self-hypnosis tapes can put drive and direction into your programing, as you will soon discover.

CHAPTER FOUR

Mind Is the Builder

You have learned that hidden hypnosis can work against you without your knowledge. Now you will discover a positive way to use self-hypnosis and let it work *for* you by making your own self-help cassette tapes. You will be using your mind to build your future. The Cayce readings advise planning your mind-building project carefully: ". . .create hope, through those suggestive forces. For mind, the builder, may bring crimes or miracles into the experience of self as well as others—dependent upon the application of same in the experience." (1908-1) Mind can be used or misused.

Offering more guidance on this, the readings say, ". . .those that use. . .those that become constructive in their thinking, that are ever constructive in their minds, in their indwellings, in their resting upon, in their thoughts, in their meditations, and *act in the same manner,* to build towards that which does make, that creates. . ." (262-78)

Self-hypnosis, or auto-hypnosis, means that you do this building process yourself. There is no middleman because client and hypnotist are one and the same. With self-hypnosis you are always in complete control because you are the one giving the suggestions and controlling the whole process. You are utilizing more of your mind and applying it in a personal, positive way. Self-hypnosis is a learning and growing experience; it is like planting your garden, nurturing it, and later enjoying the fruits of *your* work.

The first step in self-hypnosis is to discover what it feels like. The feelings of self-hypnosis can be compared to an experience you may have when doing yoga or meditating. Although meditation and self-hypnosis utilize the same basic levels of mind—and the feeling is similar— the purpose of each is different. Meditation is relaxed receptivity within the inner self, "it is the attuning of the mental body and the physical body to its spiritual source," according to the readings. (281-41) Self-hypnosis entails actively working toward your set purpose; it is your springboard for constructive change.

Other people remember this state from times when they were deeply engrossed in a television program, in a reverie, or in a book. Similarly, musicians, dancers, artists, and other creative people often become so absorbed in their work that they experience this detachment. So, start with the right attitude. Simply *let* the experience happen. Relax, but you need not *work* at relaxing.

Some people like to begin self-hypnosis accompanied by quiet, soothing background music. Background sounds—like ocean waves, gentle rain or sounds of spring in the country—are available on tapes and records. Other people enjoy a clock's ticking in the background or a musician's metronome to add beat and measure to the experience.

You can start by settling into a comfortable chair, recliner, or sofa. You may wish to cover yourself with a quilt or light blanket to prevent chilling, because your body's metabolism may slow down. Take a few minutes to settle down and adjust your breathing to a slow, relaxed rhythm. As you exhale, imagine that you are releasing all the accumulated tensions of the day. As you inhale, breathe in the stillness around you. Silence your mind and allow your body to relax. If discordant thoughts intrude, just release them.

The process takes time, but this is a special and important time for you. As you relax your body, you may notice your awareness increasing. You may find your senses growing sharper or more acute. Sounds that you would not ordinarily notice may become distractions.

Play soothing background music to mask over unwanted noise—sounds of traffic or voices in another room. Finding a quiet time of day for self-hypnosis—bedtime for instance—will reduce the chance of distractions.

Before learning to run, you had to learn to walk. And before learning to walk, you had to take small, unsure steps. So resign yourself to going slowly at first and don't expect your first sessions to produce instant miracles. Using self-hypnosis is a lot like exercising a muscle. The more you work it, the stronger it gets, and the more you will be able to accomplish over time.

Self-hypnosis begins by relaxing your body, adjusting your breathing to a steady rhythm, and allowing yourself to simply slow down. Once you have settled down, you can begin guiding yourself into a deeply relaxed and highly receptive state.

In this quiet, still time, take a moment and become aware of your body. Do your fingers show signs of curling? Are your hands tight? Are they clenched? If so, let your fingers uncurl and relax your hands. Are your legs crossed? Uncrossing them allows for better circulation. Are there any parts of your clothing or shoes that feel tight? Loosen them for your own comfort. Allow yourself to slow down a little more.

At this point you will want to relax your eyelids. A good method for doing this is counting slowly downward from ten to one and just blinking your eyelids slowly with every number. You may count silently or aloud; it doesn't matter which method you choose. At the count of one, you may close your eyes and keep them closed.

Allow this feeling of relaxation that is now in your eyes—this tired, heavy feeling—to spread outward, as in ripples or waves, to your entire facial area. Then continue to imagine this relaxed feeling going down to the rest of your body. Think of it as going first to the head...then the neck...to the shoulders...the arms...and slowly on down your entire body, step by step. This process is called *progressive relaxation* because after you completely relax one area, you go on to relax the next area.

Now, imagine some beautiful scenes or pictures in your mind. Visualize yourself at your ideal place of relaxation or any place that you would like to go to get away from it all. If you like the ocean, picture yourself at the seashore, walking barefoot on the warm sand, the rolling surf murmuring in the background. If mountains are more to your liking, imagine yourself high on a mountaintop. Hear the wind, feel how cool and refreshing it is. See the white clouds breezing by. Remove yourself from your everyday cares.

At this point, you might find your body starting to feel heavy or light, warm or cold. Different people feel different sensations, while others experience no unusual feelings at all. Some people notice a small flickering in their eyelids. This rapid eye movement (REM) can also occur when dreaming or daydreaming. Others may experience a gentle rocking or swaying motion. Like REM, this is a normal and natural experience. Still other people may experience time distortion. In hypnosis time can appear to shrink or expand. Thirty minutes can seem like five, or vice versa. And, occasionally people have an itch which they can either ignore or scratch.

With your eyes closed, you may count downward once again from ten to one, this time telling yourself that with every descending number you will become more deeply relaxed—more in perfect harmony. With practice you will discover your own timing, pace, and cadence.

Tell yourself that your subconscious mind will accept and act upon the suggestions you give it. Experience, along with the information presented in the next chapter, will teach you which suggestions are best for you. Then proceed to give yourself positive mental suggestions that affirm your ideals and purpose. With time and practice, you will achieve your optimum depth level and improve the technique of giving yourself autosuggestions. Keep these positive and to the point. Then use creative visualization exercises to see your goals and ideals already accomplished. This is how you plant the thoughts which you want to grow in the garden of your mind. This is how you reprogram old obstacles into new opportunities.

To complete the session, suggest that you will slowly open your eyes and awaken. Or count up, this time going from one to five. Tell yourself that you will feel wide awake, clear headed, refreshed and happy.

If you found it difficult to remember these steps and to *do* them at the same time you will now realize the value of a cassette recorder. Soon you will see how much easier recalling these steps will be by making your own self-help tape beforehand.

Twenty-five to thirty minutes is the average time most people give to their self-hypnosis sessions, but only you can decide how much is best for you. It is not important how much time you spend on each session, but *how many* sessions you experience. Repetition is the key. The more you do it, the easier reinforcing your success becomes.

Sometimes people wonder what is the best time of the day to do self-hypnosis. There is no definite answer to this question. Are you aware of your own biological clock? People reach peak energy levels—and low energy levels—at different times of the day or night. There are day people and night people, morning people and afternoon people. Be attentive to your own personal daily rhythm. The ideal time for self-hypnosis is that peak energy period when all your systems are functioning at full capacity. But you can also use self-hypnosis at your low energy time when you want to relax and center your scattered energy.

Enjoying your daily self-hypnosis sessions is one way of building your willpower. The Cayce readings say, "For, when the will to do is ever present and not faltered by doubts and fears that may arise in the experiences of all, then does it build, then does it attract that which builds and builds and *is* the constructive force in the experience of all." (416-2)

Though we are constantly discovering new pathways and inroads into the mind, some of the self-hypnosis presented in this book is called "traditional." It is the most common approach of hypnosis, well tested, and with an easy-to-follow formula.

Another form of hypnosis being developed recently is called "naturalistic." The medical and mental health fields are beginning to use this new approach because it is easily adapted to individual counseling and therapy.

Learning more about these two approaches will help you later when you design and write your own cycles. The traditional method uses standard procedures and suggestions that have been tested and work well. The naturalistic approach, sometimes called "clinical hypnosis," uses personalized, informal, nonspecific procedures and suggestions.

The new naturalistic method adapts the hypnosis session to the patient's needs, thereby creating better rapport between the hypnotist and the subject. This approach is gaining popularity with doctors, psychologists and psychiatrists because it helps them to see the patient more clearly, to listen more acutely, and to act more precisely.

Naturalistic hypnosis claims that a more harmonious relationship is developed by accepting the patient where he or she is and accepting his or her belief systems. Rapport is increased as the therapist listens and observes carefully. For example, if the subject says that he likes working in his garden, during the therapy session the hypnotist can use garden imagery—its sounds, smells, and activities. If another patient enjoys the ocean, the hypnotist can utilize the imagery of the sea, sounds of the surf, and feelings of the warm sand to induce a trance and as part of the visual and verbal suggestions. Naturalistic hypnosis often uses anecdotes, parables, and storytelling in the therapy.

The father of indirect and naturalistic hypnosis was Dr. Milton H. Erickson. In the book, *My Voice Will Go with You—The Teaching Tales of Milton H. Erickson,* author Sidney Rosen, M.D., writes, "In 'telling stories' Erickson was, of course, following an ancient tradition. Since time immemorial, stories have been used as a way of transmitting cultural values, ethics, and morality. A bitter pill can be swallowed more easily when it is embedded in a sweet matrix. A straight moral preachment might be dismissed, but guidance and direction become acceptable when embedded in a story that is intriguing, amusing, and interestingly told." (W.W. Norton & Company, 1982, p. 26)

It is important to note, as Dr. Sidney Rosen writes later in the same book, that "Trance, according to Erickson, is the state in which learning and openness to change are more likely to occur. It does not refer to an induced somnolent state. Patients are not 'put under' by the therapist, nor are they out of control and directed by the will of another person. Trance, in fact, is a natural state experienced by everyone. Our most familiar experience takes place when we daydream, but other trance states occur when we meditate, pray, or perform exercises— such as jogging, which has sometimes been called 'meditation in motion.'" (pp. 26-27)

The naturalistic therapist helps a person out of an old pattern and into a new mode by using every possible aspect of the client's reality. The hypnotist asks about the subject's hobbies, interests and pastimes, and observes the patient's words, the way he or she speaks and the body language.

In order to break obsolete patterns, the therapist attentively communicates with the client. He listens, watches, and then *uses* what he learns, and also observes how the subject operates. He listens to the language—not the story—and, more important, to the verbs used. The hypnotherapist then talks to the client on a level to which he or she can relate. Successful salesmen, politicians, and preachers instinctively use the techniques of naturalistic hypnosis.

People are predominantly visual or auditory or kinesthetic in their approach to life. We all have a favorite system of dealing with the world. Some of us respond best through sight, some through hearing, and others through movement. We all have a predominant system, a less predominant, and a least-used system.

Through observation, the naturalistic hypnotist determines the subject's favorite system and begins the session with suggestions geared to it. For example, if the person is visual and enjoys vacations at the ocean, the hypnotist may begin, "See yourself at the ocean, watch the waves as they curl and sparkle colors on the shore."

After a series of visual suggestions, the therapist uses the second favorite system as a bridge. To continue with this same example, let's assume that the subject's secondary system is kinesthetic. The hypnotist now uses a few kinesthetic suggestions. "Feel yourself running free on the shore and, as you run, you breathe deeper and in more perfect rhythm."

Now the therapist gently guides the subject into the *least*-used system, which automatically causes the patient to become more internal and thus to achieve hypnosis more quickly. By maintaining the person's least-used mode, the hypnotist guides the client to remain at his or her deepest level. This happens naturally because the mind has to translate information input as the subconscious goes into less familiar terrain and has to work harder.

In the example, the hypnotherapist began with the subject's favorite system, the visual; then bridged into the second system, the kinesthetic; and lastly into the least-used system, the auditory. An example of an auditory suggestion might be, "Can you hear the rhythm of the waves telling you that you can quiet down and listen now?" Much of the session will continue in the auditory.

At times the hypnotist may bridge back into the other systems, but this is the basic formula: Start with the favorite system, bridge into the secondary system, and work mostly from the subject's least-used mode.

To discover a person's favorite system, the hypnotist listens to speech patterns and watches body movements. For example, the therapist watches the verbs of the *visual* person. Here are some instances of how a visual person might speak: I "see" what you're "showing" me. That "looks" good. "Draw" me a "picture" of it. The visual person may also wave his or her hands like paint brushes. Approximately 70 percent of all people are visual.

On the other hand, the verbs of the *auditory* person will be different. I "hear" what you're "saying." It "sounds" good. "Tell" me more. Auditory people often keep their hands near their faces or touch their faces. Compulsive talkers are often auditory people, and the best way to get their attention is to use a loud noise to break into their sound barrier.

The hypnotherapist gets a feeling for the verbs of the *kinesthetic* person, who reveals himself or herself in different ways: I'm "in touch" with that. Let's "put it all together" and "work with it." The kinesthetic person is in motion; one who feels, thinks, experiences and responds to movement. Such a person operates from a feeling level, bringing the hands inward when he or she speaks, as opposed to the visual person who uses the hands in outward motions.

Naturalistic hypnosis is still new and innovative; there are no set rules. You may use some of these insights and techniques later on when you write out and design your personal sessions. As you observe and listen to yourself more closely, you will gain insight into your different systems and how to apply this into your personal cycles to enhance your mind-building tapes.

The next step, before you begin designing your personal program, is to learn and then choose the specific suggestions for accomplishing your desires. Entering hypnosis is a first step, but hypnosis alone would offer very little—other than deep relaxation and a feeling of peace and well-being—if it were not for a cycle of positive suggestion and constructive imagery geared to the accomplishment of your project. In the next chapter you will learn how to design and to word your precise suggestions for maximum success in creating your destiny.

CHAPTER FIVE

Positive Suggestion

Hypnotic suggestion is verbal instruction to the inner mind, worded so as to make it as attractive as possible to the subject. Well-designed suggestions are a dynamic way to get your subconscious to work more efficiently for you. They can regulate or eliminate habits and instill positive personality traits to help reshape your world.

Effective suggestion, like hypnosis, is both an art and a science. The science of suggestion is the actual wording —*what* is said to the subject by a hypnotist or by oneself. The art of suggestion is the *way* in which suggestions are given—the timing, tone, and cadence. The science can be learned through books, but the art is gained only through experience.

Someone once asked the "sleeping" Cayce: "In the training of the subconscious mind, which is more effective, thought or the spoken word, and why?" The answer was:

> In the training of the subconscious mind, first let it be considered as to *what* is being acted upon. Then the question will answer itself. The subconscious mind is both consciousness and thought or spirit consciousness. Hence may be best classified, in the physical sense, as a habit. Should such [a] one being acted upon be one that thinks [that] thought would act quicker

than the spoken word, then to such [a] one it would!
When it is necessary to reach the subconscious of an individual through the senses of the physical *body*, before it may be visualized by such [a] one, then the
spoken word would be more effective—and you may see
why. Hence, that which is spoken. . .to a growing, developing body in oral manner to the sleeping or semi-
conscious mind will act the better still!   262-10

The effectiveness of suggestion depends on the skill
with which it is used. Positive suggestions should induce
rather than demand, persuade rather than command.
And, above all, they should demonstrate the benefits to
be enjoyed by following them. Even in deep hypnosis
your conscience is always your guide, and you can reject
any suggestion you wish. You always have the free will to
accept or reject it.

Some people mistakenly think that hypnotic suggestion can make you do things you wouldn't ordinarily do.
Stage hypnosis demonstrations add to this confusion,
since the audience thinks that the hypnotist has forced or
tricked the volunteers into doing strange and unusual
things. Hypnosis can't *make* anybody do anything. The
people who volunteer for stage hypnosis are the type who
are very willing to do the things that are asked of them.

Although there is nothing inherently wrong or uneth-
ical about using hypnosis for entertainment, it does help
perpetuate some of the old misconceptions surrounding
it. The stage hypnotist-entertainer asks for volunteers,
knowing that the "show-offs" in the crowd will flock to
the spotlight. Volunteers for stage hypnosis are usually
extroverted and uninhibited people, those most likely to
respond to suggestions calling for unusual stunts.

The stage entertainer is adept at testing volunteers to
see how quickly they respond to conscious suggestion.
The entertainer relies on instinct, experience, and the
law of averages to find a few excellent subjects for each
performance.

The best subjects join the hypnotist onstage, while the others are sent back to their seats. Confusion may occur when the stage hypnotist dismisses some of the volunteers, since it appears that only a few of them could actually be hypnotized. But nothing could be further from the truth, for everyone experiences hypnosis at some level in its varied forms. The stage hypnotist, working against time, chooses only the best subjects, but all can and do achieve trance countless times in their lives though they may not often recognize it. For example, some recognize the alpha/hypnosis state; others don't. Though we all dream at night, some remember their dreams; others don't.

Concluding the demonstration, the stage hypnotist carefully suggests that the volunteers will not remember what they have done. Confusion again arises in the minds of some when they return to their seats and friends ask, "Do you remember all those crazy things you did?" The volunteers answer, "No, I really can't remember what happened." The friends are left with the impression that hypnosis automatically causes forgetfulness or amnesia. This is not so. The volunteers were given and accepted the suggestion that they would not remember what they did on stage. To save them from embarrassment, the stage entertainer helps volunteers to forget.

Other misconceptions date back to the early days of vaudeville. Imagine yourself for a moment in that era. A turbaned hypnotist tells an entranced smoker that his cigarettes will taste like horse manure. After waking, the smoker is given a cigarette which he promptly lights. He immediately coughs, makes a face, and quickly stomps out the cigarette on the stage floor. The audience is delighted; they think the man is permanently cured of smoking, but this is not so. He still has the need or compulsion to smoke. The only thing that has changed is that now all his cigarettes taste horrible. Later, you will be shown the modern approach for suggestions designed to end cigarette addiction.

The early days also produced uninspired results for weight control. The old-fashioned approach was to read a list of fattening foods to a hypnotized person with the strict command not to eat those foods. This technique was somewhat successful insofar as the subject did not eat the foods listed. But, in time, the person developed cravings for other foods that were not on the list and had to return for more sessions. Modern hypnosis, in newer and more effective ways, now removes the craving, the compulsion, and the addiction to overeat.

What do you think is the most important part of a hypnosis session: the depth of the hypnosis or the specific suggestions? Of course, both are important, but many people think the depth is more important. Some people will even say, "Bring me down to a real deep state," hoping they will have more success at a deeper level. Actually, effective suggestion is far more important than the depth of hypnosis. Depth has little to do with how well you can succeed in your project.

Certain people, though only able to reach lighter levels, can quit smoking completely in just a session or two. Your attitude, your ideals, and your desire to achieve results—combined with proper suggestion and visualization—are more important than your depth level. Depth can vary from person to person or even from session to session. In fact, you may even achieve a deeper level in one session and a lighter level in the next.

A few years ago, a weight-control client went home from her first session convinced she had not been hypnotized because she remembered everything about the session. She had been told (incorrectly) by a friend that, in hypnosis, she wouldn't remember anything. She might not have returned, but she noticed that she was eating less, discarding pounds, and feeling better. Yet, after her second and third sessions, she still insisted that she had not been hypnotized, even though she reported the disappearance of pounds with each visit. Trust, sincerity, openmindedness, and the ingenuity of the suggestions, more than the depth of the trance, are the important keys to a successful session.

The first rule for formulating a hypnotic suggestion is to *make it appealing*. Offer an incentive; the more beguiling the better.

If your objective is weight control, you could be left cold by the negative statement: "You will not overeat." To your mind, this statement may be boring. It's a bald-faced injunction. On the other hand, a suggestion like, "The less you eat, the better you look and feel," offers a reward: the promise of better health and a more attractive appearance.

Words like "don't" and "won't" should be used sparingly, but they may be occasionally useful when the entire tone of the suggestion is positive. "You will eat less" is far more effective than "You won't eat as much." The offer of a positive response is more likely to bring positive results—*doing* as opposed to *not doing*. The Cayce readings agree wholeheartedly and often emphasize this important point: "*Always constructive, never* negative suggestions!" (1163-2)

The challenge of designing suitable suggestions lies in the fact that there are many undesirable words that we would refrain from using. For instance, people talk about "losing" weight or "dropping" pounds. But what happens when you lose something or drop something? A rubber-band effect is created: You want to go out and find what you lost; you want to pick up what you dropped. The idea is to build a healthy, attractive body with positive words describing what you want to accomplish.

So, instead of a diet, you may start a reducing plan. Instead of denying yourself a favorite food, you can eat what you want, but in sensible amounts. Instead of "fighting the battle of the bulge," you can "fashion a slim life style." Instead of passively counting calories, you can increase your exercise activity to fifteen minutes a day. (If you are already exercising, add fifteen minutes to whatever you are already doing.) Balance your intake with your activity. The so-called starvation diets can be dangerous, but a safe and healthful way to become slim is to consume fewer calories and exercise more. Avoid junk foods. Eat healthful food in sensible amounts and drink lots of juices.

Here is a suggestion that you can use to help regulate your ideal metabolism:

> *As you exercise and eat sensible amounts of healthful foods, your body will become regulated to the ideal rate for you to become as slim as you wish to be.*

People want to change their old, worn-out habits; yet, there is at least an initial resistance to overcome in almost everyone. In the business world this kind of resistance is called "sales resistance." Sales resistance can occur when a person goes into a store intent on buying a product. The shopper wants to buy it, yet somehow, at the same time, the customer wants to be sold on it. Hypnotic suggestion is not a psychological selling game, but an effective method for bypassing mental sales resistance and unfreezing people's defenses.

Even though people truly want to change, a sense of loss is felt by some when an old and familiar habit is erased from their lives. This resistance can be rerouted by suggesting something positive to take the habit's place. For example:

> *When you think of something to eat, and it isn't time for a meal, then your mind immediately reminds you of something better, more enjoyable, that you can easily do. And it will be whatever you wish—something that really satisfies you.*

The suggestion avoids naming a substitute, leaving it to you to invent your own.

Many styles of suggestions have been developed. Some are direct and others are indirect. There are double-bind suggestions, deepening suggestions, contradictory suggestions, joined suggestions, aversion suggestions, and more. These suggestions may sound complicated at first, but actually they are simply different ways for you to communicate meaningfully with your inner mind. As you read, study, and experience these different styles, you can decide which are best for you.

If you are at all doubtful, analytical, or are used to giving orders, a subtle indirect suggestion will probably work best. Some professional hypnotists assert that a subject's occupation will disclose the proper approach. If, for example, a person is employed by the police or military, or is in any trade where he or she customarily follows orders, the direct command suggestion might be more effective.

The different approaches can be shown with a pair of illustrations. The first is a *direct suggestion* to promote relaxation:

> *Take a deep breath and let all the muscles in your body relax. Slow down your breathing. . .breathe slowly and evenly. . .relax your mind.*

With an *indirect suggestion,* the same thought is expressed as a possible consequence of something you are encouraged, not directed, to do:

> *If you take a deep breath, you can feel your body relax. And, as you slow your breathing, you can let your mind relax.*

In some instances, an indirect suggestion can use negative statements to get the desired result (negative statements are not negative suggestions). Telling you what you do *not* have to do nudges you in the right direction *to* go. For example, if you were restless in your chair, you could be told:

> *You can do anything you want. You don't have to do anything you don't want to do. You don't have to make any kind of effort. You don't even have to bother trying to move around in your chair.*

Here the indirect suggestion uses an *implication* to impress an idea just below the threshold of consciousness awareness. Unconsciously, you are persuaded to accept the notion that moving around in your chair is far more trouble than it's worth. It's an effort you must "bother trying" to make. Words like "try" are coded messages that imply failure or difficulty to the inner mind. Your inner mind interprets the signal as "It is too hard to move," and so you don't.

The next example shows how the same type of code can be inserted in a weight-control suggestion, but the principle can be used in other areas as well.

> *You don't have to bother trying to pick up that extra food or even trying to chew it.*

Your outer mind can agree easily; you don't "have to" do those things. Meanwhile, your inner mind decodes the message and programs you to regard overeating as a chore. With these and other kinds of suggestions, you can help stabilize your eating habits.

The cycles in this book are designed with both direct and indirect suggestions. As you read and use these cycles, the types of suggestions will become clearer to you.

The *double-bind suggestion* is another useful tool in the workshop of the mind. It offers alternative choices in order to counter a negative response. It is easy to say "no" to a person who asks you to sit down, but how do you answer the person who offers you a choice between the blue chair and the red one? No matter which one you pick, you'll be sitting down—whether you want to or not. In hypnosis the double-bind grants you free choice but offers you all types of possible responses:

> *Your body can feel heavy or it can feel light. Or it may feel asleep so that it doesn't feel anything at all. It can float up, or it can sink down. Or it can just very pleasantly drift. It can do whatever you wish.*

Offering a variety of options, this suggestion subtly and indirectly narrows the range of reactions.

Telling you *how* to respond to a suggestion is another important part of the psychological process. Your mind needs a rationale, *any* rationale, before it can assent. So, using a *deepening suggestion* as an example, it is not enough to tell you that you will go deeper. You must be told how:

> *You can go deeper on a count from ten to one by picturing a flight of stairs. . .(or an escalator. . .or an elevator).*
>
> *The right image will come to you.*

The objective is to involve you in choosing your own fantasy while distracting your conscious mind. With your outer mind bypassed, your inner mind, the unquestioning mind, can readily accept the premise.

Often two seemingly *contradictory suggestions* are given at the same time:

> *Your body may feel asleep even though your mind seems to be awake.*

Another technique is the *joining* of one suggestion with another whose response is assured. One example is:

> *If you take a deep breath, you can feel your body relax.*

Deep breathing tends to promote relaxation anyway, and suggesting something that is bound to happen on its own lends weight to whatever else is suggested. Even though a suggestion simply spells out the inevitable, your inner mind assumes that the suggestion coupled with the result is just as compelling.

A suggestion designed to take effect after the session is called a *post-hypnotic suggestion.* The Cayce readings eloquently define this as a "suggestion that will be retroactive in the waking, or in the physical normal body." (5747-1) The next illustration shows how *linking* a command to an inevitable activity, like opening your eyes, can enforce a post-hypnotic suggestion.

> *In a short time, your eyes will open. When your eyes open, your inner mind will realize that you are finished using cigarettes.*

Or a suggestion may be *coupled* to something that takes place when you are back in everyday beta consciousness.

> *In a few minutes, your eyes will open and you will be wide awake and comfortable. When you get up from the chair, you will know the joy and vitality of being a non-smoker, and enjoy the feeling of feeling better.*

Here a promise of reward, "the joy and vitality of being a nonsmoker," is used to enhance the suggestion's appeal. A climate of agreement is created with statements you can easily accept. While your conscious mind is nodding "yes," you are told, indirectly, that you don't have to smoke any longer and that you'll be feeling better. Years and years of advertising have made smoking seem the appealing or the sophisticated thing to do. Those years of conditioning can be neutralized, allowing you to realize that smoking is anything but glamorous.

Standing in bleak contrast to all the above positive suggestions are the old *aversion suggestions*. Aversion is a negative approach to suggestion, which aims to turn a cherished vice into an object of loathing. Many people, thinking that only the strongest medicine works, ask their therapist to "make" them hate a favorite habit by inducing revulsion whenever they feel like yielding to temptation. But if aversion suggestions were really the answer, more people would be helped by them. They are about as effective as taking two aspirin to cure a broken leg.

For some people, however, aversion suggestions may produce dramatic short-term results, yet the benefits are more often theatrical than therapeutic—like climbing a stepladder that is balanced on a rocking chair. It's really a question of credibility, as your inner mind finds it easier to believe that you feel better when you eat less.

While aversion may have its place in suggestion, it should be induced subtly and in ways to which you can easily relate. Feelings of vague distaste can be insinuated indirectly; for example, you are asked to picture yourself at your desired weight. Paint the fantasy vividly and embellish it to make it as appealing as possible. Next, visualize all the food with which you've been indulging yourself. Then you are asked:

> *Which do you want more: the new slender image of yourself or hundreds of fattening calories that your body doesn't need or want?*

Excess food is thus made to seem distasteful. If you are correcting a weight problem, "hundreds of fattening calories" would sound rather repugnant.

You have now learned something about suggestion and autosuggestion. This information will help you when you design and write your own cycles. But suggestion is only one part of your self-help program. Visualization is the next step to creating your own destiny.

CHAPTER SIX

Creative Visualization

Creative visualization, also called creative imagination, guided imagery, or seeing with the mind's eye, is another tool for programing the inner mind. Visualization is planting another seed—and watching it produce— in the garden of your mind. It is a right-brain activity, whereas logical suggestions are the seeds of the left brain.

Hypnotic suggestion and guided imagery are two of the most valuable tools in the workshop of the mind. Creative visualization adds a new dimension to thinking by using the mind's eye to picture positive actions and positive results; you can point it in the direction in which you want your life to go.

Of course, the Cayce readings contain some warnings about the use of visualization. This powerful tool should always be used in conjunction with one's spiritual ideal. It should not be viewed as a gimmick to manipulate life in order to satisfy selfish ends. But if it is used sincerely and with a high sense of purpose and responsibility, the readings promise that it can be of great help.

Visual abilities come easily to about 70 percent of all people. The other 30 percent can develop and strengthen their inner vision with practice, such as by using the cycles suggested in this book. Most people have good visualization abilities and, like a muscle, these become stronger with use. Yet not everyone can immediately "see."

Visualization covers a broad spectrum, ranging from vague fantasy images to vivid, colorful mental movies. Visual impressions can come in colored pictures, in black and white pictures, and in pictures not quite tangible. For some, it may be like a mental movie with the person as the star of the show: the person directs the scenes, actions, and dialogues. For others, impressions may come as feelings or vibrations. In their comprehensive book, *Seeing with the Mind's Eye: The History, Techniques and Uses of Visualization,* Mike Samuels, M.D., and Nancy Samuels note: "We've said that visualization is creating a mental image, creating a picture in the mind, seeing with the mind's eye. Especially when people first begin consciously to visualize, the images in their mind's eye are different from the images that they see with the aid of their retinas. Indeed, these mental images more resemble thoughts and ideas than sight. Many people feel as if they are 'making up' the images rather than seeing them. This is natural. The feeling of making it up is the way beginning visualization feels. Early mental pictures appear less vivid than external images. In fact, some people feel that they sense their inner images rather than see them." (Random House, Inc./The Bookworks, 1975, p. 121)

Some people may have difficulty visualizing because they were told in childhood not to daydream. The Edgar Cayce readings suggest, however, that daydreaming is a good pastime: ". . .the entity may lapse into what is sometimes called 'daydreaming,' and it is then given to formulate in the mind of self ideals, and even [be] able to visualize or to word same somewhat in a poetic nature." (1664-2)

The Cayce readings also recommended visualization for healing and developing ideals:

But there is not to be left out that mental attitude in the meditations of seeing, feeling the body being corrected in such measures as to fill and fulfill a greater service for creative forces and influences.   2946-1

Then, spiritualize and visualize purposes, in the manner in which the entity desires things to be done, and you'll have them done!   3577-1

Your thoughts and images *do* change your reality. The readings concur, repeating many times and in many ways, "For thoughts are things, and the mind is the builder." (281-39) As you change the thought, you change the image; as you change the image you change the reality. Creative imagination is a pathway from the possible to the tangible; it is yet another building block.

Seeing with the Mind's Eye states that "Hypnosis is one of the oldest techniques in psychology to use visualization." (p. 191) Visualization exercises are usually used for entering hypnosis, such as is shown in this suggestion:

Picture yourself mentally at your ideal, most joyful place of relaxation. . .any place that you would like to be. . .

Guided imagery can also be used indirectly; one example is:

Thoughts. . .coming and going back and forth. . .like ocean waves. Then all of your thoughts came to rest in the back of your mind, like waves settling into the sand.

Using imagery indirectly to suggest relaxation signals your inner mind that it's time to settle down. Use of the past tense assumes that the response has been given. Since you receive the suggestion in the context of its having already been accomplished, you assume that it has, and therefore it is.

Visualization is equally important for reinforcing verbal suggestion. The following direct suggestion is commonly used to help erase cigarette addition:

In your creative imagination visualize a huge black-board. On this chalkboard see the word "cigarette." Go to this blackboard and as you erase that word, you erase, cancel and completely wipe away the cigarette habit from your life. You have eliminated the need or desire to smoke. (Pause) You now have a clean slate. Return to the blackboard, pick up the chalk and, in place of the word "cigarette," write in capital letters the word "SUCCESS."

Your mind creates its own reality, and the mother of your reality is imagination. It is no secret that imagination works best when it is inspired. What better way to excite it than with a vision of a dieter's fondest dream: a slim image?

You can look into a mirror, still steamy from the tub or shower, and see yourself as thin as you want to be. Admire that reflection, realizing that is how you are going to look, now that you have discovered you can eat sensibly and be satisfied and feel good.

Creative imagery can also be used as an indirect method of realistic goal-setting:

Picture your own bathroom scales or any scales, and mentally place upon the scales the exact amount you intend to weigh.

Visualization can be used posthypnotically to bypass old impulses, as shown in the following suggestion:

Whenever you are about to eat—even when you simply think about eating—mentally picture this new, slender image of yourself and then decide which you want more: that slender, healthier body or fattening calories.

Indirectly, you are thus guided to look at that extra cheeseburger and fries as just so much fattening bulk.

You can also combine your ideals and goals into one vivid picture image. A single positive symbol can be a focal point in your visualization exercises. This single mental picture, clear symbol, or a specific emblem can add strength and focus to your creative visualization. The

Cayce readings often recommend using symbols (commercial advertisers do it all the time!) to clarify the image and the purpose: "Thus, as indicated in the emblems, these come to mean much in the experience of the entity." (1847-1)

The house of your dreams—the emblem of a happy home—could, for example, be an ideal symbol combining many of your hopes, wishes, and prayers. The readings caution, "But those that are as symbols or signs or conditions that may be used constructively, use same; do not abuse same. For that which is good, to be sure, may be used to one's own undoing." (1406-1) This means that symbols and visualization can be misused. Examples of the misuse of this faculty of the mind would be trying to gain unfair advantage over others or "making" someone love you.

In your creative imagination you can picture your goals *being* accomplished as well as imagine them *already* being accomplished. The Cayce readings often recommend seeing the suggestions being accomplished, as in the following:

> *See* in the physical structure that which is being accomplished for the body. . .   2836-2

> *Seek* and ye shall find; *knock* and it will be opened! *See* that being accomplished, and it will aid much.
> 5576-1

A good example of mentally seeing a goal *being* accomplished can be shown in this example for public speaking:

> *In my mind I can visualize myself standing in front of an audience, preparing to speak. I take a deep breath and feel myself continuing to breathe easily. Smiling, I take a moment to look at the group. I see myself as calm and vividly focus on this positive assured image in my mind.*

Seeing your goal as *already accomplished* is perhaps an even more dynamic tool for mental imagery. This is a big step toward your goal's actual fulfillment because it bridges the gap between your inner-world reality and your outer-world reality. Referring to healing, the Cayce readings state:

> . . .well that there be kept that continued attitude of *seeing* the body replenished, rebuilded, in a mental, a spiritual, and a material way and manner. This held by the body-consciousness as seeing these things accomplished, will aid *also* in the correcting in the physical forces of the body.   4482-1

Using the same example of public speaking, here is how you could apply the principle of seeing the goal *already* accomplished:

> *I now picture myself* after *the talk. People are coming up and thanking me, saying how much they enjoyed and learned from the talk. As they are shaking my hand, I realize that I truly did well. I did do a good job and am thankful for the experience of helping others and speaking with them..*

Seeing it already done says to your inner mind, "Yes, I *did*," instead of just, "Yes, I can." Here is another example of the same dynamic you can apply in a different situation:

> *If you are a student studying for a test, just imagine yourself ahead in the future. Imagine that you have already taken the test and you know that you did excellently with it. Listen to your teacher telling you what a good job you did. See yourself smiling, knowing that you did your part well. Dwell on these positive results for a few minutes. Enjoy these feelings thoroughly. Delight in the joy of fulfillment and the satisfaction of accomplishment.*

Here is another example of imaging a positive end result for creating a slender image of yourself:

> *Picture yourself the way you want to look, the way you want to be: slim, trim, healthy, and happy. Dress yourself in the clothes you'd like to wear. (Pause) Now see this as already accomplished. You are really proud of the results, the way you look and feel.*

Guided by your ideals, set challenging goals that are both realistic and attainable. Plant the seeds and nourish your mind with a vision of the reality of your goals accomplished. Get inside your imagination and feel it—place yourself inside the picture—become a living part of your inner reality. Picturing a positive end result can be the most exciting and fulfilling part of your session.

Soon you will be designing your own personal development programs using the different approaches in this book. With practice and experience it will be possible—and easy—for you to formulate your own positive suggestions and creative visualization exercises. However, a few basic rules must be remembered:

(1) Accent the positive and limit the negative. Carefully spell out what you want to accomplish, and make it appealing.

(2) Make your suggestions attractive. Stress the benefits that will come when the suggestions are followed. Suggestions need not be rigid; you may mold them to your needs and temperament. Use positive suggestions and constructive imagery to utilize and balance both your right- and left-brain hemispheres.

(3) Rehearse your new reality. Paint vivid word-pictures that show how enjoyable compliance is and how easy it is to accomplish your goal. Focus on clear mental pictures, vivid symbols, and specific emblems that you relate to personally and strongly. Listen to your inner voice, visually see and emotionally feel your goal as an already accomplished fact. This positive attitude bridges the gap between your inner and outer reality. Success comes as you combine thought, image, and action to create this new reality.

Now comes the *action* part of this book. It is hoped that you have studied well. Now is the time to apply what you have learned. Personal growth should be an enjoyable experience, so have fun building your future—today.

CHAPTER SEVEN

Making Your Own Tapes

This is the time to shift your life into passing gear and drive toward self-betterment. You have learned about self-hypnosis, applied psychology, positive suggestion, and creative visualization. Now, in three easy steps, you can combine this knowledge and begin applying it by making a personal self-help, self-hypnosis cassette tape.

Perhaps you are already familiar with commercially produced, prerecorded, self-help tapes.* Commercial tapes usually offer quality hypnosis programs at a reasonable price. It is almost like having a professional hypnotherapist in the privacy and comfort of your home, helping you to achieve your goal.

Commercial hypnosis tapes are fine in the beginning, but a better way, by far, is for you to make your *own* personal tape. You can have greater success in doing this, and the advantages in learning the process will definitely outweigh any of those offered by a purchased tape. Recording your own tape takes less than one hour and is more effective because you program it to your specific needs. By making your own tapes you will also learn more about the art and science of self-hypnosis.

---

*Some of these tapes are available from the A.R.E. You may request a books and tapes catalog by writing to the A.R.E. Press, P.O. Box 595, Virginia Beach, VA 23451.

The art of self-hypnosis concerns the timing, the tone, and the delivery—going too fast or too slow, being too forceful or too meek. The science of making a self-hypnosis tape consists of a simple three-part formula: entering self-hypnosis, the cycle of suggestion and visualization exercises, and the wake-up procedure.

You will be learning as you are doing, and you will better understand self-hypnosis as you practice it. After all, you only truly learn by doing—experience is the best teacher. You can read volumes on how to drive a car, for example, but you'll never really learn until you start driving. The car won't move itself. You have to get in, turn the key, move into gear, and then go. Theory is fine, but there is no substitute for practical experience.

The three steps for making your self-help tape are easy ones, as easy as A-B-C.

STEP A: Begin the cassette tape with suggestions *guiding you into self-hypnosis*. Some people call this stage "achieving alpha," others call it "centering." This chapter contains two separate methods for "Entering Self-Hypnosis": (1) a traditional, direct approach and (2) a naturalistic style approach. In time you can design your own method—or combine favorite parts of both approaches—for entering self-hypnosis.

STEP B: Continue your cassette tape with a *cycle of positive suggestions and creative visualization exercises*. Here is where you plant the seeds of tomorrow's bountiful harvest, where you are building your new reality—creating your own miracles.

STEP C: Complete your tape with a *"wake-up" procedure*. Some people call this "returning to everyday awareness" or "coming back to beta level." At this point you may insert suggestions for automatically going into regular nighttime sleep.

Let's look at each step individually.

STEP A: There are numerous methods for entering self-hypnosis. If you already have a method, use that; otherwise, choose "Entering Self-Hypnosis I" *or* "Entering Self-Hypnosis II."

Read at about one-third of your normal pace, and self-record either I *or* II into your cassette recorder. You may wish to play soft, soothing background music at the same time you are recording your tape. This way both your suggestions and the relaxing sounds will be on the same tape. The ticking of a grandfather clock or a musician's metronome can also be relaxing and enjoyable.

ENTERING SELF-HYPNOSIS I

(Start recording your tape here.)

Breathe deeply and smoothly for a few minutes. (Pause)

You can keep your eyes open for a minute, and you can look either forward or upward. You don't have to look at anything specific, but just look either forward or upward. I am going to count down from ten to one, and with every descending number just slowly blink your eyes. Slowly close and then open your eyes, as in slow motion, with every number. Ten. . .nine. . .eight. . . seven. . .six. . .five. . .four. . .three. . .two. . .and one. Now you can just close your eyes and you can keep them closed. I will explain what that was for and why you did that.

That was just to relax your eyelids. And right now in your eyelids there is probably a feeling of relaxation, perhaps a comfortable tired feeling, or a pleasant heavy sensation. Whatever the feeling is right now in your eyelids, just allow that feeling to multiply, to magnify, and to become greater. Allow your eyelids to become totally and pleasantly relaxed. This is something you do; nobody else can do this for you. You are the one who does it.

Just take your time and completely and pleasantly relax your eyelids. And, as you relax your eyelids, you can allow that feeling of relaxation that is now in your eyelids to flow outward in all directions, as in imaginary waves or ripples. Allow a feeling of relaxation to go outward to the entire facial area. Just think about relaxing the face. Allow the relaxation to go outward to the entire head area. Just think about relaxing the head. Enjoy the relaxation going to the neck and to the shoulders, down the arms and into the hands. Welcome a wonderful feeling of relaxation going down the entire body to the legs, to the feet, all the way out to the toes; completely and pleasantly relaxing the entire body. And you slow down a little bit. Allow yourself to slow down just a little bit. Later, as we go along, you can slow down just a little bit more.

Don't worry about any little movement in your eyelids. That is called rapid eye movement and is a perfectly normal and natural part of this experience. It will pass very quickly. And, in a moment, I am going to count downward once again from ten to one. This time, as you hear every descending number, just feel yourself slow down a little bit more with every number. At the number one, you can enter your own natural level of relaxation. I will count rapidly now: Ten, nine, eight, seven, six, five, four, three, two, one.

You are now at your own natural level of relaxation. And from this level, you may move to any other level with full awareness and function at will. You are completely aware at every level of your mind even though your body may feel asleep. You can accept or reject anything which is given to you. You are in complete control. At this level, or at any other level, you can give yourself positive mental suggestions— suggestions that your inner mind can accept and act upon in a positive manner—suggestions that are designed for your success—to achieve your goals and ideals.

See yourself relaxed in mind and in body. This is something that you want; it is here and it is now. As you take a deep breath, you can enter a deeper and healthier level of mind—more in perfect harmony, more centered and balanced—with every breath you take.

(Now insert the cycle of your choice. Wording for these cycles is found in Chapters Eight through Ten.)

ENTERING SELF-HYPNOSIS II

(Start recording your tape here.)

As soon as you are ready, you can ask yourself when you are going to close your eyes. And if you take a deep breath, you can feel your body relax; and as you slow your breathing, you can let your mind relax.

Let's begin by comparing your mind to the surface of a quiet pond. My voice can be as a breeze whispering in the trees along the shore. The pond remains smooth and calm even though things go on beneath the surface. There may be much happening beneath a still surface. You can see this image clearer with your eyes closed.

Now it is easy to dissolve the image and form another—perhaps a stairway leading down—and you can see yourself leisurely going down. The stairs can be covered with a thick plush carpet, a carpet that is like a cloud beneath your feet. Perhaps there is a brass handrail or a walnut banister. The stairs can lead you to a ballroom with sparkling crystal chandeliers, or to a comfortable room with books and crackling logs in a fireplace. And while you are here, the outside world can stay outside. You can take a few minutes and notice just how good you feel here. (Pause)

You can do anything you want to do. You don't even have to listen to my voice. Your subconscious mind can do anything it wishes, but your conscious mind isn't going to do anything of real importance here. You don't have to bother trying to listen to me because your subconscious hears with new awareness and responds all by itself.

You may be learning to recognize the feelings that accompany inner relaxation. You can experience a light, medium or deep level of relaxation; you choose what is best for you. Your body can feel heavy or it can feel light, or it may feel asleep so that it doesn't feel anything at all. It can float up or it can sink down, or it can very pleasantly drift. It can do whatever you wish. Perhaps your body feels as if it has gone to sleep even though your mind seems to be awake. Of course, you don't have to concern yourself with that.

This is a learning and growing experience. Of course, you can go very deep—and safe. Your inner mind is aware; it can hear what it needs to respond to in just the right way; it already has more awareness.

If I count from ten to one, then you can go deeper— more in perfect harmony—by picturing yourself going down a flight of stairs or an elevator or an escalator— any pleasant image you wish.

And if I count from twenty to one, you can go twice as deep, enjoying a pleasant, comfortable feeling—any kind of feeling you wish. Twenty, nineteen, eighteen, seventeen, sixteen, fifteen, fourteen, thirteen, twelve, eleven. . .ten, nine, eight, seven, six, five, four, three, two, one.

As you relax, take a deep breath and slow down, you can go deeper. As you enjoy the comfort, you will note that there is less and less importance to my voice. You may find yourself drifting to your ideal, joyful place of relaxation.

(Now insert the cycle of your choice. Wording for these cycles is found in Chapters Eight through Ten.)

STEP B: The cycles in this book are a full-brain activity that include both positive suggestions (left brain hemisphere) and creative imagination exercises (right brain hemisphere). After reading the cycles, decide which one you wish to start working with. There are 31 possible cycles to choose from in the next three chapters.

Immediately after recording "Entering Self-Hypnosis I" or "I," continue your tape by reading the cycle of your choice (see Chapters Eight through Ten) directly from the book onto the tape. Depending on your pace and the cycle you choose, your completed tape will be approximately one-half hour in length. Use this tape once or twice each day for one month.

Achievement can happen at any time. It can happen immediately or you can experience it later on. Subtle changes may usually begin in a few days and substantial changes experienced within a few weeks. Some people respond quickly to the message of their tape, other people slowly and carefully change and grow, step by step, day by day.

You develop your will to succeed by making your tape and using it daily. Dare to believe in your new reality. Live it, reach deep inside yourself, and touch it. Act in ways that are consistent with your new becoming. Show the world the new you by thinking, speaking, acting and living this new reality.

As you study the cycles in the next chapters, you will notice that some are worded in the first person ("I realize that abundance is a good thing and that I am worthy of it"), and other cycles are worded in the second person ("You can do anything you want to do"). Some cycles are a combination of first person and second person. Decide which approach is best for you and adapt the cycle accordingly. And, of course, you may change or adapt any part of any cycle to fit your personal preferences or specific needs. If you add suggestions, remember to keep them positive and to the point. In time you will be designing and writing out your own cycles, the suggestions for entering into self-hypnosis, and the wake-up procedures.

STEP C: After the cycle, complete your tape with the wake-up exercise or procedure. Self-hypnosis is not sleep, so you do not really "wake up." But "wake-up" is an easy way to explain the process of returning to everyday beta consciousness. Since you are completely aware during your self-hypnosis session, you would automatically awaken if an emergency arose that needed your attention. But the slow counting-up process, combined with proper suggestions, gives your mind ample time to adjust and orient itself to the everyday world.

WAKE-UP PROCEDURE

(After the cycle, continue your tape here.)

Your conscious mind may forget to remember all that you accomplished here today. But your subconscious mind always remembers. It is already acting upon these suggestions and these visualized images in a positive manner. Benefit—success—can come at any time. It can come back with you now, or you can experience it in due time. And, in a little while, when you return, you will feel just wonderful. But before you come back here, be aware that you can drift back clear-headed—that you will be wide awake, refreshed, and happy.

I will count from one to ten, at the count of ten you will open your eyes, be alert, energized, and feeling fine—feeling better than before. I will count now: one. . .two. . .coming out slowly. . .three. . .four . . .coming up now. . .five. . .six. . .feel the circulation returning and equalizing. . .seven. . .eight. . .awakening your full potential with perfect equilibrium and normalization throughout your being. . .nine. . .ten. Open your eyes. . .wide awake and feeling great.

(Your tape is now completed and ready to use.)

Because self-hypnosis is so relaxing, if you play your tape at night you may find yourself drifting off to nighttime sleep before your tape is finished. This is fine. The subconscious mind is always aware—always listening and absorbing information. But if you want to take a more active part in your tape session, *sit up* in bed or in a chair and lie down only after the session is finished.

You may also find your conscious mind wandering while you are listening to your tape. This is perfectly normal and natural, because your conscious mind isn't doing much of importance at this time. For this reason, it is very important not to use your tape while driving an automobile or working with any dangerous equipment.

If you are specifically planning to use your tape *at bedtime,* you may prefer not to include the wake-up procedure, but to insert instead suggestions for progressing into your regular nighttime sleep automatically. Many people find this a wonderful way to go to sleep at night without the use of medication.

PROCEDURE FOR GOING INTO NIGHTTIME SLEEP

(After the cycle, instead of the wake-up procedure, *continue your tape here.)*

As you begin to think of what was just said moments ago, your mind begins to pleasantly drift. You may feel yourself—or see yourself—beginning to gently drift into regular, restful, normal and natural nighttime sleep. The drifting can come as in waves, and at its own pace—bringing with it a wonderful sense of well-being and harmony in mind and body and spirit. You may hear your inner voice reminding you to awaken in the morning, at your usual time, refreshed and happy. You are calm, quiet, and in perfect balance as if in a dream—dreaming of yourself dreaming.

(Your nighttime tape is now finished and ready to use.)

You can record one side of your cassette tape, ending it with the "Wake-Up Procedure" for daytime use. Then record on the reverse side the same cycle but substitute the "Procedure for Going into Nighttime Sleep" and use this side at bedtime.

Occasionally some people will say that they don't like the sound of their own voice on tape. It is important to realize that everyone hears his or her own voice partially through the bones that run from the jaw to the ear. You never accurately hear your voice as others hear you, except on tape. You can improve the projection, the quality and the cadence of your voice through practice by talking into a tape recorder. You can hear yourself as others hear you and adjust your voice accordingly.

A cassette recorder is a small investment for the potential benefit you can get from it. But if there are absolutely no recorders available, read out loud the cycle of your choice as a daily meditation. If it is at all possible, however, do purchase or borrow a recorder. Once you are experienced in making positive programing tapes for yourself, you might consider showing members of your family or friends how to make *their own* tapes and this is truly "helping people to help themselves."

It has been said that "It is better to light one candle than to curse the darkness." The next three chapters contain 31 cycles that are like 31 candles to light up your life. Read the cycles and then decide which project you *want* to start with. If your doctor has told you that you *must* stop smoking, for example, but you don't truly *want* to, then wait up on that project for the present. Start first with a cycle that you really want to do—like "Attracting Love," "Self-Health" or "Developing Psychic Ability."

The 31 cycles are all very different. They vary as to style, approach, and format. Most were originally designed by professionals, some were the ideas of just ordinary people that have been further developed to make them applicable for general use. Some are in paragraph form, others in poetry form. (The subconscious mind responds well to the cadence of verse; i.e., verse and symbols seem to be the language of the subconscious.) The wide variety of cycles is presented to give you numerous examples and models from which you may design *your own* cycles. Before each cycle there is a short introduction explaining it.

Chapter Eight contains cycles for daily living and growing. These are practical cycles that can help you achieve specific goals and personal success in many everyday situations.

Chapter Nine's self-care cycles are for bettering your health and appearance. They are pathways to self-improvement and health by helping to eliminate self-destructive habit patterns and attitudes. Other cycles are designed to enrich your appearance and ease stressful situations. All of these cycles are an investment in *yourself*.

The cycles in Chapter Ten are for touching a larger consciousness. These special cycles were specifically developed for your spiritual growth and understanding. Exploring life's innermost secrets, you can expand the frontiers of your mind and flow with the rhythm of life. There is no shortcut to perfection, but these cycles can help you on your path to experiencing fully the human adventure.

Editor's Note: The last cycle in Chapter Ten, "Healing Sound Cycle," is presented in full; i.e., it includes the procedure for entering hypnosis plus the wake-up procedure along with the regular cycle. The reader, then, can see what a complete self-hypnosis session would look like.

CHAPTER EIGHT

Cycles for Living and Growing

1 PREPARING FOR CHANGE

Many people who have worked with the different cycles in this volume have said that this one is perhaps the most important. Change is what rut-busting—getting unstuck—and positive programing are all about. The only time we cease to change is when we cease to live. And then, who knows? Death may be the time when *real* changes begin.

After making her own tapes and using the different cycles, this is what one woman wrote to say: "The most important thing that comes to mind for me is the cycle, 'Preparing for Change.' I think, after one has done all the working with self-hypnosis, that the cycle of change should most definitely be used to start with. If it does nothing more than let your mind become free to accept and work with the inevitability of change, then you are that much ahead in the game of living. For, once people accept that changes come—no matter what their form—their entire lives and most definitely their attitudes will evolve. It is certainly a release from stress. In fact, the one true value of working with the change cycle is the relief and release of stress from one's system—mentally, emotionally and physically."

Change *is* inevitable. This cycle is dedicated to positive change and will help prepare you for life's uncertainties. Truly, *this* cycle is a great place in which to begin being more in control—and less a victim—of life's many ups and downs.

Preparing for Change Cycle

(Continue your tape here.)

I feel a need for change—in my body, in my mind, in my soul, and in my emotions. I am ready to accept life's continuing process of change, forming a new pattern to learn and grow, welcoming change in all levels of my life.

As I prepare for this continuing process of change, I will remember and analyze past changes and observe that each change was a lesson to be learned and was necessary for my growth. As I continue to study past changes, I will realize that often what were the most challenging changes were, in truth, the *greatest opportunities* for my personal growth.

And, in dealing with human emotions, I realize that in the past I may have felt I was the victim of change. But now I am the instigator of change. Now, rather than meekly waiting for change, I can and will initiate change. I can make it happen. I will fill my changing with a positive and realistic attitude and accept that each change brings with it levels of growing that are necessary and good for me to experience.

I understand the need for constant change and self-betterment. I can visualize this as a home which has not been cleaned, repaired or remodeled, but has been left to deteriorate. Or as I would look upon a neighborhood which has not progressed, but has fallen apart. Or even a city or a nation which refuses to change and becomes stagnant. This process of change is ongoing, up and down, through generations of peoples, eras, and seasons. Sometimes there seems to be no "middle ground," no safe place to avoid change. This is especially true with me, so I will plan on progress, I will welcome change, and I will build my future.

Change must come into each life, as day must follow night. What I *do now* determines what my changes will be and how I can grow with them. I bring my goals and ideals together into one vivid symbol or picture of how I will grow and become stronger and more loving. The right image will come and I will focus on this clear picture.

The greater and more profound the changes, the greater and more dynamic is my strength to meet these changes and grow through them. I release and set free the burden of negative emotions, whether self-inflicted or not, which I have felt from persons or events in my past. I release the feelings which I have imposed upon myself and held. As I forgive and bless other people—and release these emotions—I feel better and more positive about myself. I am confident in the future I am planting. The seeds of my tomorrow are in my thoughts, my plans, my words, my touch, and my actions.

I wholeheartedly embrace the joyous responsibility of change in my life by liking myself, by taking care of my body, by letting my emotions grow constructively and by lovingly sharing my joy with others. In the eternal *now* I am making me a more positive person. I bless those who have taken care of me in the past and those who will share my life in the future. I give and receive blessings each day and grow to be a happier, more loving person with each season of change in my life. And, I bless myself for caring about myself and my growth.

I develop my will to change and my will to succeed. I have created a new habit of joyfully welcoming change at all levels of my life. I appreciate change, for it brings new opportunities for positive action.

I am thankful for the many positive changes which have already happened within me, around me, and through me. I am thankful for the exciting changes yet to come. I welcome them, knowing that the continuity of life is change. I am becoming all that I am capable of being.

(Complete your tape with the wake-up procedure.)

2 BUILDING SELF-CONFIDENCE

Have you ever wondered why some people seem to be successful and happy, while others seem to be unhappy and to fail in whatever they do? Have you noticed that some seem to have the Midas touch, while others, even with plenty of money and a good education, seem to struggle all the time? What is this difference between people who merely get by and those who excel? What is this "winning edge," this inner strength and confidence?

Take time to observe both groups of people carefully. Listen to their words. Basically speaking, those who *expect* to succeed generally do; those who lack courage and constantly complain often fail. This observation may be too simplistic but, if you take the time to study people, you will generally find this to be true.

Did you ever know a successful, self-assured person who expected to be a failure? Probably not. Did you ever meet a person who thinks and speaks only of failure who ever became a great success? Again, probably not. When you think about success, you become successful. When you think confidently, you become confident.

The subtle seeds of self-confidence are *already* within you. This cycle nurtures those seeds so that they may blossom and be fruitful. Not only will you overcome shyness and doubt, but you will also learn your body's signals in reaction to stress, anxiety, and nervousness. Most important, you will be shown how to redirect your body's natural adrenalin into controlled energy.

"You win when you expect to win, you succeed when you expect to succeed" is probably one of the great unwritten laws of life. With a little effort, you *can* expect to do great things by using this cycle.

Building Self-Confidence Cycle

(Continue your tape here.)

There are some things you can learn about yourself.
One of the things you can discover is that you can be the person you want to be,
but you don't have to be the person you don't want to be.
You can find your own way to discover your abilities.
Of course, it is possible to question whether you can do something even though your subconscious mind knows you can do it.
It is possible to discover your abilities,
to rely on yourself,
to let your subconscious give you the positive,
right information which permits you
to do the right thing, at the right time.

It is possible for you to learn that what seems like nervousness is, in reality, adrenalin.
Adrenalin is a substance manufactured by your body during times of stress to help you meet the challenges of any stress situation in which you might find yourself.
Controlled adrenalin is energy, positive energy for your body.
Some people may feel that this energy seems like nervousness, but it is possible for you to begin to understand that what seems like nervousness or stress is energy—positive energy you can consciously direct in any constructive way you want.

You can recognize and learn your body's signals.
And, as you learn your body's language,
you begin to consciously use your ability
to experience within yourself any assured positive
feeling you wish.
As you recognize your ability to be assertive,
you will see and hear the word "confident"
forming within your subconscious mind.
By mentally repeating the word "confident" as often as
you like, your mind helps you do all the things
you have to do.

If you take a deep breath, you can have
a very pleasant daydream of yourself—
relaxed, composed, and alert—
speaking and acting with calm self-assurance,
secure in your own knowledge
and sharing this knowledge.
Possibly a sense of electric energy surrounds you.
You can recognize this energy as controlled adrenalin,
reminding you of your ability to use all your skills
to achieve whatever you wish.

In this daydream you can see and hear your mind repeat
and echo these words:
"I am a winner; a confident, successful, goal-oriented
winner.
Others may be willing to sit back and wait for things
to happen, but I am willing to work to *make* things
happen, because I am a winner.
I can vividly picture myself as confident and
in command.
I focus my thoughts on this image, this positive symbol
of inner strength.

I remind myself that my mind creates my reality,
and this is the reality my mind is now creating. (Pause)
I see and feel this as already accomplished
and picturing it as already having happened.

I succeed when I expect to succeed.
I am healthier when I expect to be healthy.

I am confident by making a habit of thinking
and talking and acting in a confident way.
I actively search out ways to be helpful,
to be constructive in word and action.
I find reasons to praise honestly and intelligently,
to give credit where it is due.
By looking for the good and the positive,
I encourage and praise others
and, especially, myself.

I write my goals and ideals clearly on a piece of paper and
carry it with me. Clearly defined, written goals are tools
with which I build my new life. Goals are like a map that
gives direction to where I am going and shows me how I
am going to get there.
My goals and ideals are my winning edge.

With daily habit, I reaffirm my objectives and strive for
them in a positive way. With this persistent striving, I
take new pride and joy in my growth and success. My
accomplishments are both exciting and rewarding."

(Complete your tape with the wake-up procedure.)

3   MEMORY AND CONCENTRATION

Do things seem to slip your mind somehow? Do your
thoughts wander and are you easily distracted? Is it difficult for you to concentrate fully on what you are doing?
Some people find that the harder they try to concentrate,
the more difficult it is and the more frustrated they become. This cycle can help you change that pattern by focusing your attention where you want it.

Self-hypnosis for improving memory and concentration is especially helpful to students. They can learn
more material in a lesser amount of time. (This seeming
expanding or shrinking of time is technically called *time
distortion*.) They improve their grades by increasing the
speed with which they learn and, at the same time, have
better retention of the material. Even foreign languages
are easily learned with help from this method. Not only

students, but world travelers and business people use self-hypnosis as a study aid in learning other languages. You can do this also. Here is how:

Records and tapes for learning foreign languages are available commercially or you may borrow them from your library. Your added edge will be to play the record or tape a few times while you are in a self-hypnotic state. Give your inner mind the suggestion to record and retain the information until you need to retrieve it. And, even though it could be many years later when you are in a foreign country, the words you learned will be there when you need them.

This cycle can help you improve both your memory and your concentration. You'll enjoy using your mind to increase your awareness, and you'll think more clearly and creatively with less effort. Concentrate on doing this cycle right now before you are distracted.

Memory and Concentration Cycle

(Continue your tape here.)

The time you spend learning and studying
can be shortened,
or it can be lengthened.
You can learn a great deal in a few seconds,
or you can spend hours learning little.
All that is important for you is to decide
just how much you want to learn and how quickly.
Sometimes subconscious learning is all that counts.
You can condense your learning
into a short and intensive time.
You can acquire knowledge and store that knowledge
until the moment you need it.
You can hear something and record it.
You can see something and record it.
You can read something and record it.
You can feel something and record it.

You can experience something and record it.
You can "picture" the things you read.
You can "hear" the things you see.
You can "feel" the things you hear.
You can "experience" all that you study.

It isn't important what you recall right now,
but it is important that you recall it when you need it.

It is all recorded in your inner mind.
You can quietly remind your inner mind:
"Whenever I study, my mind is like a camera.
Everything I see, I remember.
Whenever I read, I mentally record what I read.
I listen and see and feel as I read.
My mind is like a tape recorder.
Everything I hear, I record.
My mind is also like a video camera.
Everything I see and hear, I program on tape.
My inner mind records and stores
all images and sounds for my later projection.
I experience all that happens and record an impression
of it.
I recall and retrieve as I desire.

I have an excellent memory.
It is easy for me to learn and to remember,
because I can focus my mind on anything I like,
for as long as I like.
Sustained concentration strengthens my mind.
When I exercise my memory, it becomes stronger
every time I use it, every time I study.
I have clear, quick thoughts
and specific retention of information.

I have instant replay and long-term replay of
information.
Memory and concentration enhance my capacity
for a more successful, creative, and productive life.

I can program thoughts, facts, and information
into my inner mind,

and let my mind record and store this information
for my future use.

I can add feeling to the information I program
to make it more alive, vital, and important.
By relaxing, I can bring this material back
to my outer mind.
The information has been processed.

(Now, if you are a student studying for a test, just
imagine yourself ahead in the future. Imagine that you
have already taken the test and you know that you did
excellently with it. Listen to your teacher telling you
what a good job you did. See yourself smiling, knowing
that you did your part well. Dwell on these positive
results for a few minutes. Enjoy it thoroughly. Delight
in the joy of fulfillment and the satisfaction of
accomplishment.)

(Complete your tape with the wake-up procedure.)

4   ATTRACTING ABUNDANCE

Everyone wants something—be it something physical, emotional, mental, or spiritual. But we don't all want
the same things; some may want only enough to get by;
others want it all. A happy medium lies somewhere in between, and this happy medium can be termed *abundance.* You can decide exactly what abundance means to
you and you can develop an abundant state of mind—a
wealthy "mind-set."

Many people just want more money. They may or may
not know what they want to do with it, but it is more important to decide what they will do to get it. Very little
comes with no effort. You need to do the work in order to
achieve the goal. This cycle is an excellent way to start
the work. Use it daily, and then go out and do something
about it.

Prosperity begins in your mind, and this cycle is your
opportunity to use your inner mind creatively to produce
abundance. Some people may say, "My financial situa-

tion is such that I need a miracle." Yet, you are entitled to miracles. Positive programing is how to begin to make them happen.

Abundance can come in many forms. Money is only one. Your life may already be more abundant than you realize. Not only can you increase your abundance, but you can become more aware of the abundance already in your life.

Attracting Abundance Cycle

(Continue your tape here.)

What is abundance to me? As I evaluate material success, I realize that abundance is a good thing and that I am worthy of it. I perceive that I am entitled to life's many blessings. But to me abundance is much more than merely money or things; abundance is in having good friends and in being a good friend. Abundance is a harmonious life, a music-filled home, creative work, a meaningful relationship, quiet inner peace with strength and spiritual growth. I will enter into a new age, and for me this new age is the age of abundance.

I see abundance all around me. In nature—in the fields and the forests, the rivers, the seas, deep within the earth and high in the sky—there is abundance for all.

I feel abundance in and around me. It is here and it is now. I welcome this abundance with joy and delight.

In my creative imagination I see an economic healing happening. It seems a miracle! I have been blessed with abundance. I have opened an inner door and stepped into the sunlight of abundance in all its manifestations. And I say "thank you" for this great gift. For I know that it comes, not from me, but through me. And with this new abundance, I can grow and serve that I may be a channel of blessings to others, for abundance is an expression of love.

I have tuned in to the aura of abundance that surrounds me. Like the electromagnetic field of a magnet which extends beyond the magnet itself, so it is with my energy field, reaching out far beyond the actual physical me. And, as a magnet, it draws abundance to me. It attracts and guides me to abundance. And this I now do:

To attract abundance I now act and think as one who already has abundance. I smile often and easily. I enjoy taking time for the little things and the quiet things in life. I walk tall and proud and perhaps just a little faster now. I have many exciting new habits reflecting this abundance.

To attract abundance I take good care of my physical appearance. But I take even better care to balance my inner appearance. I am aware now to choose my spoken words carefully, but I am even more considerate of my unspoken words. I use positive, cheerful words easily and often, for they reflect the profound, positive, cheerful feelings deep inside of me.

To attract abundance, I praise others for the good that they do. I compliment others honestly and sincerely. I thank others lavishly. I compliment and thank myself also, and welcome this new me. I like listening attentively to others, and they enjoy listening to me.

To attract abundance, I find meaning and joy in the work that I do, my activities, and my service to others. Work is love in action, so I happily do more and contribute more than I am paid for. My creative work is a pleasure and a fulfillment. But, if my present job is void of creativity and promise, then I can analyze the alternatives and take the steps necessary for a rewarding new career in whatever field I choose.

To attract abundance, I carefully make lists of my goals, my ideals, and my plans—especially my plan of action. I write out in detail what I will accomplish, how I will accomplish it, and when I will accomplish it. I make realistic short-range goals and I make reasonable long-range goals. And then I simply go out and do it, and I often believe that I am far ahead of my goals.

To attract abundance, I make friends and associate with positive, creative, and active people, for I realize that I am always influenced by the people around me and with me. So it is vital that I choose wisely those with whom I work and play, live and love and grow. Positive, happy people encourage me and inspire me as I encourage and inspire them.

To attract abundance, I clean out all excess clutter in my life. I phase out all trash. I give away my neglected things that others may use them. I make room for the many, many blessings coming my way. I joyfully bestow my blessings by sharing my excess abundance with others. And, as the useless and the unwanted depart, I experience the freedom and the lightness of an unburdened life. What then comes in to fill the void spaces will be a joy and a delight.

To attract abundance, I allow myself to laugh often and to laugh loudly. My sense of humor has expanded into a habit of laughter. With happiness and laughter, I attract new friends, positive people who laugh and enjoy life with me. With joy and laughter, I improve my health and appearance. I laugh and the world laughs with me. I make people laugh each and every day, for laughter is like an internal massage.

To attract abundance, I open my doors wide when opportunities knock and I welcome them with open arms. My life now is exciting and active, and many, many blessings come to my door. If nothing succeeds like success, then nothing is more abundant than abundance.

I open the door to the joyful discussion of abundance.

I open the door to my actions and thoughts of abundance.

I open the door to my caring for my outer and inner appearance.

I open the door to praising others and myself.

I open the door to new joy in my creative work.

I open the door to listing my goals, ideals, and my plans for action.

I open the door to expanding my world of friends.

I open the door to releasing the excesses in my life.

I open the door to joy and laughter.

I open the door to the new me—today—now, and it is so!

In my creative imagination I can see a clear, sharp image of myself attracting abundance. I take time to review my ideals and goals. (Pause) I hear friends congratulating me on my successes. (Pause) I feel a total enrichment has already been accomplished.

Now I realize the great secret of abundance: Abundance is not an end in itself, but a growing process, the result of my creative work and efforts. I have learned from the past, make plans for the future; but live in the eternal now. I already have abundance and, by the joyous welcoming and sharing of abundance with others, I increase my abundance a hundredfold.

(Complete your tape with the wake-up procedure.)

5 PUBLIC SPEAKING

If you have ever stood before a group or performed in a school play, you already know that uneasy feeling. Almost everyone has experienced "butterflies" before. "Butterflies" quite accurately describes the feelings when adrenalin is triggered and pumped through your body to deal with a stress situation.

This cycle has helped bashful and reticent people become excellent public speakers. It can help you become a confident, effective speaker—perhaps even a verbal dynamo. When you are given an opportunity to speak, use this cycle a few weeks before the scheduled event.

Public Speaking Cycle

(Continue your tape here.)

I can be anything I want to be.
I can really understand how to feel good talking to other people.
I am becoming an effective speaker.

Emotion is a good thing;
it is an element of being human.
I enjoy that element, but emotion is not enjoyable
if it prevents me from expressing myself openly
in a clear, logical way.
If there had been times in the past
when, through emotional stress, I may have been
unable to communicate easily,
I realize this *was* all in the past.

Now that I am becoming an effective speaker,
I understand that the inner feelings
which I may have experienced are simply adrenalin—
my body's own abundant, natural energy,
available for my use,
available for me to harness and control
at the right time
to accomplish any goal I set for myself.

Controlled adrenalin can keep me sharp and aware;
I can direct and channel it into enthusiasm and vitality.
I can become whatever I want to become,
and, with this realization,
I am becoming a successful public speaker.
I allow my own innate sensing mechanism

to let me do the right thing at the right time,
to let me say the right thing at the right time.

I speak clearly, precisely, calmly, and effectively
in a way that people can enjoy and easily relate to.
In my mind I can visualize myself
standing in front of an audience,
preparing to speak.
I take a deep breath
and feel myself continuing to breathe easily.
Smiling, I take a moment to look at the group of people.

My thoughts are coming into focus,
they are distinct and well organized,
because I am cognizant of what I am going to say
to get my point across.

I am an effective speaker;
I am sure of myself
because I have prepared my material and am familiar
with it.
I see myself as calm
and vividly focus on this positive assured image in
my mind.
(Pause)

I am an experienced speaker, expressing myself
delightfully in every situation.
This is an enjoyable and exciting experience
because I concentrate on what I am giving to the group.
I clearly deliver each important point to my audience.
I am simple, yet direct.
As I am speaking to the people,
I am loving them and serving them—
giving my gifts—
aware of what I am sharing,
helping them to learn and grow.
Expressing the full and profound
magnetism of my soul.
I feel this as having already been accomplished.
I am thanking the audience for this opportunity to share
and be with them. (Pause)

I now picture myself *after* the talk.
Smiling people are coming up and thanking me,
saying how much they enjoyed and learned from the talk.
As they are shaking my hand,
I realize that I truly did well.
I did do a good job and am thankful for the experience
of helping others and speaking with them.

(Complete your tape with the wake-up procedure.)

6   ATHLETICS AND SPORTS ACHIEVEMENT

Mentally rehearsing the plays before a game is not a new idea, but subconsciously playing the game and already seeing it won—while in hypnosis—is a novel and profound one. Many top athletes "psych" themselves up by using self-hypnosis. A casual reading of current sports magazines will give an idea of how hypnosis techniques are being applied by players of your favorite sport. For example, some professional teams who have hypnotherapeutic tapes in their mood rooms not only use hypnosis for motivation but also for revitalizing their physical bodies. Tapes help ease their physical aches as well as instill psychological well-being and enthusiasm.

The greatest enemy for any athlete is fear: fear of losing, fear of winning, fear of pain and injury, or fear of humiliation in public. Some athletes who play beautifully at practice will freeze up during a game while under scrutiny from others. This pressure can often inhibit a good performance.

To perform well, an athlete must be relaxed enough to allow the natural timing and coordination to flow with the movement of the game. When he or she is in the flow, every movement feels right. The critical and doubting mind can be bypassed to allow the athlete to experience the fullest potential. Above all, a playful sporting attitude helps the participants to realize that it is a sport to be enjoyed.

This cycle is designed for both competitive and non-competitive sports; the separate suggestions are clearly marked. It uses a combination of first- and second-person suggestions, and will help you to fine-tune your concentration and allow you to use better your body's natural adrenalin. This is a high-performance cycle.

Athletics and Sports Achievement Cycle

(Continue your tape here.)

You can fine-tune your concentration as you would fine-tune your automobile to get it to run at peak performance. You are learning, at an inner-mind level, to adjust your attention to your desired objective. As you gear your energy, you can shift yourself into overdrive when the need arises. And you are also learning to shift back down to cruising speed once the event is over.

The secret of all athletics is practice, practice, and more practice. In addition to practice on the field, you can practice playing in your mind. Mentally rehearsing at an inner-mind level gives you that added edge, the winning edge. You can carefully think what is best to do *before* an actual game, just as you think during the game. And you can think after an event, not as self-criticism, but planning how you can do better next time. As you center your thoughts, you automatically center your actions.

You are learning to use your body's own natural adrenalin for alertness and control. Adrenalin is manufactured by your body to give you extra strength in times of need or when you want high performance. You can use it at will. It is high energy, naturally, and you can turn it off after a great performance.

At this time you can mentally repeat—or echo in your mind—the following positive suggestions:

**EDGAR CAYCE FOUNDATION and
A.R.E. LIBRARY/VISITORS CENTER**
Virginia Beach, Va.
OVER 50 YEARS OF SERVICE

I concentrate as I'm playing and I rehearse mentally
between games.
My body realizes what is best for me, so I use my energies
naturally, with my mind in control.
I can perform at peak, always better than before.
By relaxing before an event, I can focus on the goal.
I am fine-tuning my mental concentration and physical
abilities.
My coordination improves whenever I practice (insert
the specific sport you are working on: running, golf,
tennis, etc.).

Now take a few minutes and just imagine yourself
excelling in this athletic endeavor. Create in your mind
a single positive symbol for success. (Pause)

You are what you think you are. You become what you see
yourself becoming. Just imagine that it has already
happened, that you already are a high-energy performer.

(For competitive sports.)

Mentally see and hear a crowd of people cheering your
game and your success. You can hear them saying what a
great play you made, and *you*—more than anyone—
realize that you did well.

You excelled and you won because you did your best.

If you are part of a team, see yourself as an integral part
of the team effort. See yourself as one of the pistons in an
engine running at peak performance.

(For noncompetitive sports.)

See yourself simply enjoying your sport as an
invigorating experience. It is pleasing to be doing it and
you enjoy the exercise and renewed physical health.
Listen to the rhythm of your body as it keeps pace with
your movements and deep breathing.

(Complete your tape with the wake-up procedure.)

7   CAREER PLANNING

Do you ever feel unfulfilled in your work? Do you wish you could change your career? Do you wonder what you would do instead? Many times your attitude can make the difference between just a job and a fulfilling profession.

This cycle can help you find the best direction ahead. But don't be surprised if you find more than one opportunity awaiting you. Some people can, and do, have a couple—even a few—careers at the same time.

By learning how to make maximum use of your spare time, you can open yourself to life's many opportunities. Some people even develop hobbies that can become profitable businesses, such as antiquing furniture or growing house plants.

Your age need not be a limiting factor. Some very young people have good businesses going and some senior citizens accomplish a great deal. Remember Grandma Moses, the famous American artist, who *began* her career when she was 78 years old?

Your future is wide open. You *can* be anything you want to be.

Career Planning Cycle

(Continue your tape here.)

You can be anything you want to be.
But you don't have to be anything you don't want to be.
You can consciously choose to do anything you want to do.
Or, in due time, your subconscious may guide you to endeavors that utilize your natural inner abilities.
At this level you begin to discover innate talents and inner knowledge that can be applied to any area of your life.

Some people need ample time to realize their inner gifts.
Other people have so many natural talents that they
need time to decide which ones they wish to pursue
actively.
Some people hurry in pursuit of a career, when often
they need but to be still, to listen first,
and be open to life's opportunities.
By carefully choosing to slow down your outer mind,
you gain new awareness and guidance in your
inner mind.
Some people write out a list of things they plan to do,
and a list of things they wish not to do.
Like a patient fisherman, some people cast out their lines
in many directions to see from which places responses
come.
The wise fisherman knows that though there may be no
response one day, the very same spot may be alive the
next day.
Life is like fishing; with persistence and patience,
all things are accomplished.
What you are doing now in your spare time gives insight
into what you will be doing later on.
Time, even spare time, is an energy to be used wisely.
As you breathe in and quiet your thoughts,
new insight, new directions form deep within you,
symbols of your new self.
It doesn't matter if this is perceptible to you right
now or not.
All that is important right now is that you have a deep
desire to apply yourself in a brave new way, that you
want to step out of old ruts and worn patterns.
As you dare to believe, as you trust in life,
as you listen to your subconscious,
you realize that your future is determined
by the careful and wise choices you make now.

In your creative imagination, look ahead and see
yourself near the autumn of your life. You are older
and far wiser now, more experienced, and can review
your entire life from this perspective. As you mentally
look back upon your life, ask yourself, "In what way

do I wish to be remembered?" "Have I served and helped others?" "Have I been honest in my dealings?" Especially ask, "How have I used my life?" and "Am I pleased with myself?"

Your higher self truly knows the best directions. You can follow its lead and act upon your inner feelings. Your inner self becomes your best authority. Soon you will really understand what the best directions in life are for you. Follow them.

(Complete your tape with the wake-up procedure.)

8   DEVELOPING A SENSE OF HUMOR

Smiles and laughter are the universal language of humanity. Who can resist the smile of a child or a kind and friendly wit? We all can enjoy a little more humor and levity in our lives.

Humor is fun—and it can be healing. A well-known author, Norman Cousins, used humor as therapy and overcame a major illness. From his sickbed he watched hours of slapstick comedy; this was his way of dealing with pain as an alternative to medication. His book, *Anatomy of an Illness,* is now required reading at Harvard Medical School.

Humor can also be used for spiritual development and for good health. Cayce once advised: "At least make three people each day laugh heartily, by something the body says! It'll not only help the body; it'll help others!" (798-1)

A sense of humor can help you find joy and fulfillment in your daily life no matter where you live or what your circumstances are. Not only is humor the reflection of a happy soul, it is a way, a means of sharing life's joys with others.

Humor is a profound and creative force. This cycle can encourage more of the joy and laughter that is *already* within you. Allow joyfulness and merriment to become a pleasurable habit and a way of life.

Developing a Sense of Humor Cycle

(Continue your tape here.)

At times I have taken myself and my world too seriously.
And at other times I burst forth with laughter and joy.
How special are the times when I simply let go
and roar a hearty laugh.
What great release and expression!
Sometimes I have laughed so much
that my sides seemed to split,
and this causes more laughter, and I just
let my body laugh even more when this happens.

I feel better after a good laugh.
Laughter is good for my body—
it is like an internal massage.
Today I express a little lightness,
a bit of levity,
a smile, a cheerful word,
a hope, a song of joy—
and this becomes a pleasurable habit,
a positive way of life.

Sometimes I am most comical
when I take myself too seriously.
Humor balances the extremes of my life
and puts things in proper perspective.
When ego becomes punctured or puffed,
if I plop to a depressing low,
I'll just smile and laugh—and let it all go.
Humor is my saving grace
that helps me to laugh at myself
and see my all-too-human folly.

My eyes and my mouth express my humor,
and my face radiates with joy—
but my face merely reflects
what is already within my mind and heart.
Humor and joy begin within
and express outward.
I look for the funny, the silly,
and even the ridiculous.

A smile is said to be one of life's greatest assets.
It can work miracles
by transforming me, by relieving tensions,
strengthening bonds and brightening my outlook.
I am forming a positive habit
of smiling often and smiling with delight.
Smiling costs little and pays well.
Smiling expresses humor,
grows into laughter,
blossoms into joy.
Joy is my expression of appreciation and thankfulness.
My joy is alive with profound creative force.

In my creative imagination I am picturing how positively
the world responds to my smile and my warm humor.
I am visualizing how good I look and feel
when I smile and laugh.
My laughter is a positive symbol of my happiness. . .
joy is an emblem of my life;
laughter builds love, and humor affirms my humanity.
The picture of this already accomplished is very clear.

(Complete your tape with the wake-up procedure.)

9   ENDING A RELATIONSHIP

We learn and grow through our relationships with others. When we love and trust, we expect a relationship to last forever. Yet there may come a time when a certain relationship must end. Times change and people change. Those who have met our needs in the past may no longer meet them now. Nothing lasts forever. We learn to flow with life's beginnings and endings.

Endings are sometimes unpleasant. They can be sad and difficult even though they may be what's best for all concerned. Later, however, you will be a stronger and a wiser person for the experience.

This cycle is designed to ease the pain of parting, but it also opens the door to positive new opportunities. There is new excitement waiting; there are places to go, people

to meet, and different things to do. You will learn to live
your life as fresh and new, and to live each day more fully.

Ending a Relationship Cycle

(Continue your tape here.)

Shakespeare said, "All the world's a stage,
And all the men and women merely players.
They have their exits and their entrances. . ."*
Sometimes people visit our lives
and, while they are here, we can welcome them
and enjoy their company
and carry happy memories of them when it's time for
them to go—even when it seems there may be some
disappointment attached to it.
You are beginning to learn that life
is like a drama.

By turns the curtain rises to open an act—
the curtain comes down to close an act—
but the play goes on,
with new actors and new excitement,
and all kinds of wonderful experiences to enjoy,
places to go, people to meet and different things to do.

I wonder if you can imagine a curtain being raised
and everything is changed.
Now the set is different, a new scene is beginning—
with possibly a pleasant sense of excitement and
anticipation—as you discover all the things that are
waiting for you.
Perhaps you can pretend you've just come to the earth,
and life begins with your next breath,
and everything is fresh and alive.
(Pause)

You know how to remember certain people, certain
experiences, even though at times it seems you can
forget them.

As You Like It, Act II, Sc. 7, l. 139.

You know how to remember.
Now you can begin to discover that, in due time,
you will think of [him/her] less often,
but always with pleasant recollections
of happy times you shared—
blessing the passage of this relationship
and all that you have learned from it.

Very soon now, something new is going to happen.
You will meet someone,
and day by day [he/she] will take up more of your
thoughts.
Sometimes you may even try to think of your past
relationship and discover that your thoughts
go to this someone new and special,
someone who is even nicer,
who brings you happier feelings,
whom you are truly more deserving of.
And you will learn again just how exciting
a new discovery can be.

The old act has ended.
And, by turns, the curtain rises again,
for you have earned the right to experience
and enjoy a better relationship.
Imagine your life all fresh and new.
You live each day fully,
learning from the past without regretting it,
as you enjoy today;
looking forward to your tomorrows with happy
expectation.

The curtain opens; you take your place and
the action begins.
In fact, it has *already* begun.

(Complete your tape with the wake-up procedure.)

10   FINDING LOST OBJECTS

Perhaps you have misplaced items at some time or another. Perhaps you were in a tizzy for hours or days wor-

rying about it. Perhaps you finally found the item, perhaps not. This cycle presents a new way to approach an old problem. This particular cycle may not be in your "high priority" category, but it is presented to give you ideas and insights about using more of your mind in novel and interesting ways.

Self-hypnosis can help you speed the process of searching and at the same time ease your anxiety. The finding of lost objects has been shown to be highly successful when the procedures are carefully followed. A special suggestion is given to the inner mind to find the missing object in a certain way, at a certain time. This takes all the pressure away from you and speeds recovery of the item. Use this cycle if you misplace something special.

Finding Lost Objects Cycle

(Continue your tape here.)

Before looking back on time and events,
you can allow yourself to become completely relaxed.
In your creative imagination
mentally visualize the misplaced item
and see yourself as having already found it—
perhaps right where you originally set it,
or where someone else subsequently moved it.
All that is important now is that you "feel" and reunite
yourself mentally with the article.

Literally feel it back in your hands,
and avoid thinking about just "how,"
but just do it.
Simply feel it;
sense it as if it is already here.
(Pause)
Take your time.

As a detached observer, you may start going back
through time to before the article was misplaced.
You'll discover that it is easy and pleasant to do this.

Reliving is always interesting—
a pleasant, enjoyable exercise.
Slowly look around and sense the place and time;
this is your time to retrace your actions.
At this deep level of relaxation,
this higher level of awareness,
it is easy for you to re-experience.

Take your time; take all the time you want,
and slowly review the chain of events as you see them,
as you feel them.
Realize that some people see a memory, others hear a
memory, and still others feel or sense a memory.

All that is important now
is that it is interesting for you to recall or relive
events of the day, step by step,
or in slow motion,
as you follow along, understanding what you did,
how you did it, and why.
As you tune in to the events, using your mind
as a mental zoom lens,
focusing in on the exact scene and activity,
the more vivid it all becomes,
seeing pertinent actions and clear pictures.

In a little while—when you awaken,
as you get up—
in due time you can go and recover the item.
Much to your amazement, the object will not be
in the first place you search,
but you can discover it
at the second place you look.
You will be pleased with your success
and thankful for the return of your goods.

(Complete your tape with the wake-up procedure.)

11 ENHANCING CREATIVITY

Each side of your brain—each brain hemisphere—
controls certain activities or processes. Your left hemi-

sphere is concerned with verbal description and suggestion; it is your "practical" side. Your right hemisphere
is the side of creative visualization and mental imagery;
it is the seat of your intuition, musical and artistic ability,
and even your sense of humor.

The self-hypnosis cycles in this book use a full-brain
approach; that is, a combination of both verbal suggestion and creative imagination. This cycle, however, is
specifically designed for right-brain development: The
suggestions are not as "clear cut" or as specific as in the
others. This cycle will help more of your creative potential to unfold. You can use it to remember your dreams, to
listen to your hunches, to daydream creatively, to discover hidden talents and abilities, and to have more insight
into all that is around you and in you.

Your creative right hemisphere is the full-blown sail
of your mind. The practical left hemisphere is the rudder
that helps direct your course. Allow your adventurous
creativity to propel you and use your guiding rudder to
keep you on course. A marriage of your right brain to left
brain is the ideal in any creative endeavor. Balance your
full potential by verbally discussing your creative insights with yourself or with others.

One good method to develop your creativity is to play
a favorite piece of music, then—while in a self-hypnotic
or reverie state—verbally describe out loud, using all
your five senses, a memorable vacation or a pleasant
event in your life. At another time, play different music
and imagine a story—make up a story—aloud, that fits
the mood of the music. This "stream of consciousness"
exercise bridges the right and left hemispheres.

You can also use creative daydreaming by taking a
short break during the day to quiet your body and envision in your mind your ideals and your goals. Thomas
Edison regularly took "cat naps" and often awakened
with new insights and ideas. He wrote these ideas in
countless journals and on scraps of paper; then he dis-
cussed these ideas with people close to his work.

Enhancing Creativity Cycle

(Continue your tape here.)

If you take a deep breath and exhale it very slowly, you can visualize your breath like the ocean with the waves coming and going. And, as the waves ebb and flow, so does your breath come in and go out. Allow yourself to rest upon the shore, and imagine all the weight leaving your physical body. Imagine yourself beginning to float safely, bit by bit. Allow yourself to float comfortably a little bit more above where you are resting. Enjoy this wonderful feeling of rising up and pleasantly floating on the air.

As you are enjoying this feeling of floating, you become more aware of your inner self. You can visit parts of your inner self and look into the deep recesses of your mind. You can look on things from your past and gain knowledge and learn—positively. Allow yourself to sense and feel rather than merely think. Your heart and your emotions are doors to your creativity. Allow your inner knowledge—your stored memories—and hidden talents to unfold through your feelings and emotions, for through the avenue of the heart you gain new insight and inspiration.

Begin to feel the quiet radiance of light and life surrounding you. Let yourself hear the harmony that is you becoming in tune with creation, with the spirit within. Be still and listen to this inner voice; it tells you of new awarenesses and new perceptions.

Your inner voice encourages you to enter your special Creativity Room. You hear your inner voice saying: "This is my ideal space for growth and development. I come here for inspiration and insight. This is my inner place to be intimate with my creativity. I have access to a wealth of information and talents. I detach myself and redefine my perceptions."

In this Creativity Room your inner mind creates mental images, clear pictures of creative insight. The right image will come to you. Create a symbol of your success. These creative insights can also come in on their own—any time, day or night. Symbols come through dreams or sudden flashes; and, because they can be subtle and fleeting, you can have pen and paper ready to write them down. Exploring the dream state, you better understand the symbolism and simplicity of your inner wisdom.

Your nighttime dreams and your daydreams can bring new inspiration and expression beyond your present understanding. Look within to these creative insights, visions, and illuminations to discover more fullness of life. Picture yourself and feel yourself using this creative process. Spell out your objectives, and then wait and listen to the voice and symbols of the inner self. Allow creative mind to give you the answer. Answers can come quickly or slowly.

The more you use this creative process, the quicker and easier it all becomes. You will think beyond your present way of thinking and act beyond your present mode of action. You are already using more of your creative potential—it is already happening. Utilize this creativity and bring it back with you, as a symbol, a stream of consciousness, or a new way to do things.

You can slowly return from your venture upward. Returning, settling gently and softly back on the beach, watching the waves and the sea.

(Complete your tape with the wake-up procedure.)

12   THUNDERSTORM APPRECIATION

Overcoming fear of thunderstorms may seem an unusual use for self-hypnosis. But this cycle is presented as an example—a model—of how you can design a personal cycle for alleviating other fears and phobias. This cycle was originally designed by a woman who was working on a special project, and this is how *she* approached it. You can use the same basic procedure and approach it *your* way, in your own style. These basic procedures can be adapted and used to soothe almost any common fear and phobia.

If you are disturbed by the violent—but natural—phenomenon of thunder, this cycle can help. In the past there was very little you could do, except wait until the storm passed. Now there is help; self-hypnosis can make the difference. But don't wait until the middle of the next tempest to start using it. Prevention is the secret. Start now and be prepared for that next storm.

Thunderstorm Appreciation Cycle

(Continue your tape here.)

Yes, thunder is loud.
Its booming seems to go right through you,
and flashes of lightning are unexpected.
This is something you are already aware of.

Perhaps there was a time long ago in your past,
perhaps when you were a very small child,
that there was a severe thunderstorm.
Being so young and inexperienced, it was natural for you
to be unsure of something you couldn't understand.
But you knew something was happening.

All of a sudden the world became dark,
and loud sounds filled the air.
Unexpected light came from nowhere,
and the wind rushed through the trees.
Children look to the adults in their lives
to explain their world to them.
Naturally, you looked for assurance from those close to
you that everything would be all right.

Perhaps there was no one there to explain
this natural phenomenon to you,

and to tell you that "Yes, a thunderstorm is powerful and
intense, but there is an inherent beauty in it as well.
Nature is cleaning the air and putting on a light show,
complete with sound effects."
It could be that the adult with you at that time
had an unreasonable feeling about storms
and could not assure you and calm your feelings.
Whatever the reason or situation,
that was long ago and in the distant past.
Here and now with your present understanding
you can take another look
and feel better about changing your perspectives.

All that is important is that you are willing to change.

Sometimes old feelings actually create
more stress than the thing feared.
Fear can be good when it allows caution in your life,
so you don't take foolish chances.
By understanding and restructuring your thought
patterns you can create feelings of a healthy respect
for nature.
It is time to change the pattern.
Visualize and feel yourself actually enjoying nature's
light show.
Let the heavens declare their majesty;
it is for your listening and visual pleasure.
Focus on a clear picture, create a vivid
symbol that brings a new message to your inner mind.
Involve new feelings and positive emotion—
plant a new seed.
It has been said that there has to be rain
before there can be a rainbow, so use the
rainbow as your emblem of success, your goal-image.
(Pause)
And feel this feeling of ease as already accomplished.

(Complete your tape with the wake-up procedure.)

CHAPTER NINE

Cycles for Health and Beauty

13 SELF-HEALTH

The earth's seasons—spring, summer, autumn, and winter—are also the seasons of life. All life has a natural cycle of birthing, growing, maturing, and dying. A person, a relationship, a family, a home, a community, a city, or a nation that is not growing is, in fact, declining or dying; as Bob Dylan sings, "He who isn't being born is busy dying." That point where growth and completion peak is so delicate that it is hardly noticeable; there is almost no real balancing point between growth and decline.

Your body is like your home; you need to maintain it. You cannot have a bright and cheerful home unless you let lots of fresh air and sunshine into it. Self-health can result from letting thoughts of joy and good will enter; like the song says, "Let the sunshine in."

One secret of a long life is to continue growing, reaching, and changing. If you are physically weak, start exercising your body. If your thoughts are weak, start exercising your mind. A person once asked Mr. Cayce in a reading, "How can people avoid aging in the appearance?" Edgar Cayce answered simply. "The *mind!*" (1947-4)

Self-hypnosis *is* healthful and natural food for the mind. Nourish your mind as you nourish your body, for there is no better healer than positive thought to dissipate the ills of the body. Your mind is the key to healing, regeneration, and a healthy glow. If you desire a robust, strong, healthy body, then think health and you will bring health.

Self-Health Cycle

(Continue your tape here.)

See yourself floating in a vast, infinite, shoreless sea of glowing white light, an essence gentle as a morning mist. This is your own consciousness, your own mind, and you are learning to guide it, to make use of its healing energy.

Feel this gentle healing light. Allow it to spread softly throughout your entire being. Bathe every muscle, every cell, every atom in soft, glowing healing energy.

This healing light is alive within you and radiates from the deep recesses of your silent memory. Feel the warmth of this healing glow, its radiance—quiet, gentle, timeless. Feel it flow in gently spreading waves over every part of your body. Sense it growing brighter, stronger, warmer; bringing strength and vitality, excitement and happiness.

Self-health is mainly a matter of mind. You are what you think you are. And you are now learning to restructure old attitudes. Strong, happy thoughts build a strong, happy body.

Because good health is chiefly a state of mind, you can now consciously and subconsciously think healthy. Thinking healthy, you act healthy. Acting healthy, you become healthy. Illness prevention and sound health begin with attitude. You are what you eat, drink, and think. Choose carefully. A change of diet will not help you if you do not change your thoughts.

Using the mind to consciously control the body is not a new idea. Eastern yogis, martial artists, and philosophers have been doing it for centuries. If you consciously control your thoughts and direct your mind in more tranquil directions, you can perceptibly influence heartbeat and blood pressure and reduce muscular tension.

If worry, fear, anger, or depression strikes, the body reacts physically to what is essentially an emotional upset. Under stress, blood pressure soars, muscles tense and cramp, the stomach stirs, and the heart beats faster. All of this, of course, disrupts the body's equilibrium and weakens its resistance.

On the other hand, your body can now respond positively with a sense of peace and happiness. It can be relaxed, radiant, and alert. Medical science now recognizes that many common ailments originate in the mind, and often the most effective cure is the one that reconditions old attitudes. To perfect your body, start by perfecting your mind. To beautify your body, beautify your mind.

As you program a healthy attitude, you realize that your body is the home of your mind and spirit. Your mind has the ability to repair its home as needed. Your mind and spirit are able to rejuvenate your body.

The more you exercise your body, the more quickly it rejuvenates. Your attitude helps control how old you let your body grow. With sensible exercise, healthful diet, and a positive attitude, you can actually feel your body begin to feel younger. Rejuvenation is the act of becoming younger again. You have the ability to rejuvenate your body and heal the healer within yourself.

Spirit, mind, and body are parts of the whole. An imbalance in one part creates blocks which affect other parts. Therefore, use your inner mind to create a spirit of health and to build a sound body. Your body is the servant of your inner mind.

Mind is the builder. Mind can build your body as your hands can build your home. Start with a strong foundation and design a comfortable appearance. Your body, like your home, can reflect your creative desire. Build carefully.

Because every great achievement begins in the mind's imagination, you can use your imagination now to begin constructing a healthy new body. You have begun the process of rejuvenation and regeneration.

If you form a mental image of yourself as you intend to be, you will feel healthy and happy and be filled with energy and stamina. Enjoy this picture of vibrant good health. Keep it foremost in your mind. You *are* healthy, energetic, and able to perform your physical activities. Hold this image or symbol of good health. (Pause) Imagine that it is already accomplished, and experience a feeling of feeling better. The information has been recorded.

Now tell your mind to make this vision reality. Tell your mind to make it happen; your mind can do it. What were once only wishes, you can now translate into reality. You are aware of this because you are doing it even now—keeping your mind happy and your body healthy.

Healing happens on a physical, emotional, mental, or spiritual level—or it happens on all of these levels at the same time.

(Complete your tape with the wake-up procedure.)

14   STRESS MANAGEMENT

Is your life a perpetual-motion machine? Do you feel

that you are driving through life in the second gear of a three-speed automobile—wound-out tightly and working hard? This cycle is designed to help you shift into high gear and make the going easier and smoother.

Everyone probably needs a certain amount of stress to grow and develop, but *managing* the many stressful situations in life is the goal of this book. Everyone experiences stress in one form or another—physical stress, mental stress, emotional stress, even spiritual stress.

This cycle uses traffic as a metaphor. But, because stress affects different people in different ways and at different times, you may wish to design this specific cycle to fit your personal needs, using this only as an example. Change the metaphor, the suggestions, and the visualization exercises for your particular situation.

A relaxation break is like a pause in the chatter of life. A football player on the field must often take several steps backward to avoid being tackled, and yet he proceeds toward the goal. You also can learn to take a step or two backward to catch your breath and gain new perspective before making your moves.

Stress Management Cycle

(Continue your tape here.)

As I realize that I am now deeply relaxed, I can also achieve this relaxation at other times and places. When I take a few minutes and close my eyes, I can re-experience this calm feeling whenever I wish. And, as I practice this daily, this calmness, this harmony, becomes a part of my life.

When I close my eyes for a few minutes and, stepping back, take a deep breath, I can mentally say and repeat the word "relax." I then achieve internal centering or quieting. This simple exercise helps balance my actions with my thoughts and my

thoughts with my actions. And then, the more
demands that are put on me, the more strength I have
when I open my eyes and, stepping forward, meet the
situation.

Through these moments of quiet that I am practicing,
I am understanding myself and others better. I learn
to rise above stressful situations by working toward
the best solution and not being held down by the
problem or by my real or imagined fears of it. I am
learning to keep my ideals and goals always in sight
by focusing on the greater good to be achieved beyond
the obstacles.

I am experiencing harmony on a physical level, a
mental level, an emotional level, and a spiritual level.
As I step toward peace and fulfillment on each level, I
become a happier, healthier, more loving person—
stronger within myself—and, therefore, more able to
cope with the world.

As a mental exercise, I can imagine myself as an
automobile. I can start my day, as I start my car;
then, slowly and carefully, I shift into higher gear. I
am aware of the traffic and the conditions around me.
I take the best roads toward my daily objective and
make careful choices at new intersections. Most of the
time, I cruise in high gear, but I'm aware that at any
time I can shift down to a slower speed. I control the
flow of energy at all times.

And when my day is done, I reverse the process and
start slowing down. When in the morning I geared up
my speed, now I gear myself down to a quiet idle. For
now my work is done and I tune down the engine.
Now I take time to reflect on the day and be thankful
that I did the best I could.

I visualize myself as always in complete control,
aware of what I'm doing and why. I see myself taking
short relaxation breaks during the activities of the
day. I hear friends and fellow workers telling me how

calm and yet more efficient I have become. I feel myself taking a few minutes to step back and think before doing a new job so that I need not waste time or steps. Then, I feel myself step forward and carefully use my time and energy in the most efficient ways. I plant in my mind a vivid image or symbol of my success, and I experience this goal-image as already accomplished. I am picturing a positive end result.

After taking daily relaxation breaks, I am far more dynamic and productive when I open my eyes and take action. The more I am asked to do, the more ability I have to do it with and do it in a calm, assured, and positive way.

(Complete your tape with the wake-up procedure.)

15   SEXUAL FULFILLMENT

Sexual fulfillment begins with sex education. Edgar Cayce, through the readings, was a leader in the holistic (healing the whole person) health movement; he was also a forerunner in sex education. In one entire reading, dated July 10, 1935, he spoke of the need for sex education, explaining that problems in this area came from "the lack of education in the young *before* their teen-age years" (826-6) because few have a proper understanding of what the biological urge produces in the body.

The readings say that the places to begin are in the home with the proper education of the mother and father, and in the schools with the teaching of young people. The reading continues:

> . . .for public education, there should be the greater stress laid upon the educations in these directions; and not wait until they have reached or arrived at that position where they begin to study physiology, anatomy or hygiene. But even in the *formative* years there should be the training in these directions. . .   826-6

Sexual fulfillment is also learning about one's self and one's body, as well as feeling comfortable with the

naturalness of the body's arousal emotions and responses. This cycle helps develop the mental attitude so
necessary for a totally pleasurable sexual life. Sex does
begin in the mind with proper education and—barring a
biological dysfunction—can be improved by one's
thoughts. If you have a specific sexual ideal, you can design a more personal cycle using the suggestion and visualization procedures outlined earlier in the book.

This cycle has helped people find fuller expression of
their emotional needs by dispelling unreasonable fears
and inhibitions. People have commented that it has
helped open (or has restored) a healthy flow of communication between them and their partners. Sexual fulfillment comes also from the heart, as sex can be the ulti-
mate embrace of love and trust between two individuals.
A time of quiet meditation, music, or massage before and
after lovemaking can add to the spiritual qualities of the
experience.

Sexual Fulfillment Cycle

(Continue your tape here.)

If you are a healthy, active being, it is possible for you
to discover your total sexual abilities. With new
understanding, you can develop a positive mental
attitude toward all aspects of an exciting sexual life
and a harmonious relationship with your partner. By
really understanding and being comfortable with
yourself, you do not have to try to fit yourself into
somebody else's mold. You can be happy knowing that
you are *you,* at ease and confident with your body.

Trust your feelings and inner judgment as you
discover and perfect your approach and style. Sexual
growth is a learning and sharing experience and, like
love, it grows and develops. It becomes more beautiful
and more fulfilling. You can calmly enjoy and
appreciate each physical experience as an

experience—without trying to analyze or compare, doubt or brag, beg or promise. All you really need to do is slow down and savor the experience as a normal and enjoyable experience.

Instinctively your body knows its own needs and in due time will fulfill them. By using pleasure as your guide, you discover and enjoy once latent desires and abilities. You gain confidence and fulfillment by being creative in your passion. You gain new insight through observation. You can ask yourself questions: "When is passion most enjoyable—day or night?" "Do I prefer dim lights or scented candles, music or silence?" "What is my body saying to me?" "How can I be more understanding?"

People guide each other by learning to grow together—no rules regulate what they choose to share. Lasting satisfaction is not a race to be won or a competition to see who finishes first. For some, the goal is not necessarily orgasm; the real goal is in tender touching, gentle words, and intimate embrace, for fulfillment comes also from the heart. Often the greatest joy is not just in the doing, but by being playful together and truly enjoying each other.

The mutual giving and taking of affection is the secret of sexual harmony. Because there are no time limits, you can take hours for your lighthearted and your serious loving. Perhaps share a glass of good wine and a full body massage while playing your favorite music. Be at ease with yourself and each other. Discuss your needs and wants and, as important, what you enjoy giving and doing. Talk together freely. Touch lightly and touch deeply.

In your creative imagination, envision the kind of relationship that you want. See yourself balanced with equal amounts of give and take, doing and accepting, speaking and listening. Joy and happiness become the symbol and the rhythm of your life.

Clearly visualize you and your partner sharing love, making love. Feel the waves of response. And, most important, see yourselves *after* lovemaking. Picture this afterglow as the most pleasant part, an emblem of togetherness and peace. Feel yourselves hum with satisfaction and fulfillment.

You are pleased that you both enjoyed each other. In your mind you may hear yourself or your partner saying, "Wow! That was wonderful." And it was. Feel this as already accomplished, and be thankful for the sheer joy of being alive and together.

(Complete your tape with the wake-up procedure.)

16   OVERACHIEVERS

It has been said, in jest, that the slogan of the overachiever is, "Thank God it's Monday!" To strive, to accomplish, to succeed is good, but like all good things, it can be overdone. Most people need and appreciate gentle nudges in their lives to overcome inertia; others need a rest to slow down and take time to appreciate the fruits of their work. To accomplish is good; to rest is also good.

Sometimes overachievers double their speed but lose aim of their direction. This cycle was designed to give high-energy people a rest. What is amazing is that, as they slow down, they can later accomplish more with less effort. There is nothing better than taking a rest time to give new perspective and clearer insight.

An active life has momentum, and the achiever uses this energy to his benefit. But as goals are reached and successes won, it is important to shift down into a lower gear, or at least cruising speed, instead of overdrive. This cycle makes that possible—and easy.

Overachievers Cycle

(Continue your tape here.)

Take a deep breath and breathe out.
Feel yourself relaxing.
Hear the words "calm" and "relaxed"
echoing through your being.
You are calm and relaxed,
you are feeling wonderful.
Imagine, now, soothing bath water slowly covering you—
gentle warmth enveloping you—
first, your feet, then your legs,
your stomach, your chest, neck and head.
You are calm and totally at peace.

You are breathing easily and naturally as ever;
all cares are absorbed into the water,
and you are totally limp.
Every muscle is soothed by the subtle rhythm of the water
as it lulls and caresses every inch of you.
You're floating, lighter than you've ever felt before,
allowing the water to take you here and there
with its gentle flowing motion—
in and out again,
soft, rolling, soothing,
quieting your mind,
separating you from all pressure and responsibilities,
cradling you in peace and harmony,
in a place that is totally filled with tranquility.

Flow with the gentle lapping of waves on a sandy shore,
being a part of that action, a part of the water,
feeling rhythm of constant harmonious ins and outs.
Now, with a count of ten to one,
you will become even more relaxed and at ease.
Ten...nine...eight...seven...six...five...four...three...
two...one.

You are a goal-oriented person.
You have many plans and projects to improve your work
and your life.
You are a high-energy person and you love life.
You take pleasure in living life to its fullest each day;
and, because of this natural, exuberant energy that

you have, there are times when you may have forgotten
to allow your body to rest fully.

Life is filled with ups and downs, a balance of summer
and winter, of rain and sunshine.
You need both the highs and the lows
in order to understand this balance.
You may have become preoccupied with one aspect and
neglected the other.
This is easy enough to understand.
Perhaps you have been driving yourself too hard
in order to achieve a specific goal.
But now you realize that balance is in order,
because intense driving and pushing
actually delivers a reverse effect.
Built-up kinetic energy feeds on itself,
until it can spurt energy in random directions.
But this was in the past. Now you simplify your life.

You are understanding your energy patterns now
and are able to harness, control, and release your
life's energy in exactly the way you want to.

Look at yourself closely.
Note the instances when you experienced this state
of overabundant energy.
You can realize that this oscillating energy
was at times wasted and counterproductive to your
needs and goals.
Whenever this feeling comes,
take a moment to close your eyes and count from ten
to one.

Feel the tension releasing,
and feel your body relaxing into its normal equilibrium,
your maximum productive state of calmness and poise.
Give yourself, allow yourself, this moment of diversion,
this relief from all efforts and mental pressures.
Simply feel relaxed,
and now it will be easier than ever
to organize and synthesize your plans and activities,
because you've renewed yourself

and given your body needed rest from physical or
mental work.

Now it will be easier than ever to handle your
responsibilities more effectively than before,
because you can be whatever you want to be.
You can calm yourself
and relax your mind and body
whenever the need arises.
You can also set time aside each day, each week,
for the enjoyment of your many successes,
and make time to appreciate your blessings.

Even after this session is over,
each time you count from ten to one, with practice
you can enter this same state of calm relaxation
that you are experiencing right now.
Recognize and rejoice that you have such abundance
of energy at your disposal
and realize that it is easy to harmonize this energy
and balance it in such a way that it allows you
to attain maximum benefit.

Picture yourself as the calm, relaxed person
you wish to be.
Experience this as already having been accomplished
and know deeply that you *can* be anything you wish to be.
You can be calm, relaxed, poised, and in control of
your energy in every situation.

(Complete your tape with the wake-up procedure.)

17 YOUR SLENDER IMAGE

Is maintaining a comfortable weight a struggle for
you? Is your life a constant see-saw of weight gain,
weight loss, weight gain? Have you tried most of the fad
diets? Self-hypnosis may be your answer because it
works at a mind level—not a mouth or stomach level—
and your weight is determined by your mind.

The only safe and sure way to control weight is by exercising and by changing your eating *habits*. You may

have struggled with elimination diets which are sometimes self-defeating. These diets stress what you *cannot* eat, setting up an inner conflict that can enforce a craving. A better approach is to eat three balanced meals; eating things you like—but in sensible amounts. With self-hypnosis, your inner mind can regulate what is a sensible amount for you.

There are no magic pills, no special sweatsuits that have any lasting effect, until you change your way of thinking first. A slim body begins with slim thoughts, just as a healthy body begins with healthy thoughts.

This cycle will help you take off weight quickly, easily, naturally, and permanently. You can create a new attitude of yourself as slim, healthy, and energetic.

Your Slender Image Cycle

(Continue your tape here.)

You have been eating much more than your body either needs or wants. And you, the mind, controls eating—not the stomach, not the mouth; no, you, the mind. You are beginning today at this same mind level to program yourself, to develop new habits, and to set new goals. You are laying the mental foundation for the new you, a cheerful and attractive you, the you that you always knew you could be.

Of great importance to this positive new you,

to your healthy, active and attractive body,

is the fact that the less you eat, the happier you feel.

The less you eat, the more you smile.

Now the less you eat, the more relaxed you are.

Now the less you eat, the better you look.

Now the less you eat, the more patience you have.

Now the less you eat, the more motivation you have.

Now the less you eat, the more energy you have.

Now you find satisfaction in eating less. You can pride yourself in knowing that each time you do eat less, you are rewarding your slimmer self: the self you want to be, the slim self you are becoming, the slim self that you *already are* deep within. Whenever you choose this new image of yourself, you experience new feelings of health and well-being. It feels good to feel good about yourself.

The most amazing thing is that each day now, in your eating habits, you are forming new patterns. Each day now it is easier and easier to eat sensibly. You are gaining new strength, and that strength is the ability to eat sensibly. You can eat sensibly and still be satisfied.

As you exercise that new strength, it grows; it becomes more able, more fit. And each day now, as you eat sensibly, this becomes more and more reinforced, more a natural part of your life. It is like using the muscles of your arm: As you use them each day, they become stronger. As you eat sensibly each day, it becomes easier and easier to continue in a practical way, a sensible way.

Eating sensibly means that you mentally ask your own body what foods it needs. Then, quietly listen to your own body, and it will tell you what foods it wants and needs for you to eat sensibly, nutritiously, and happily. Eating sensibly is eating slowly and carefully, always concentrating on chewing, always thinking of that mouthful that you are chewing. Eating sensibly also means drinking sensibly, drinking more fruit and vegetable juices.

As you exercise and eat sensibly, your body will automatically be regulated to the ideal rate for you to become as slim as you wish to be. By using your creative imagination, you can picture yourself as you would like to be. You can create a positive mental image of yourself as exactly the way you want to be, as exactly the way you want to look. Mentally dress yourself in the clothes you'd like to wear. Create a vivid symbol or mental picture and hold it foremost in your mind. (Pause)

You can see yourself increasing your physical activity by fifteen minutes a day. Listen to yourself breathe better as you are regularly doing and enjoying your favorite exercises. See yourself using your new energy in a positive, constructive way. Feel this new energy going throughout your body, building a healthy new you. Feel how it feels to be slim, trim, and healthy.

You can picture your own bathroom scales or any scales and mentally place upon the scales the exact amount you intend to weigh. (Pause) Just imagine that it has already happened, that you already weigh this amount, that you have already increased your physical activity, that you already look the way you once wished you could look. At one level, you already are this positive you, and you are *really* proud of the results—the way you look and feel.

As you think healthy, you become healthy. Health is an important part of the new you. Breathe clean air, eat sensible food, experience normal daily eliminations, and keep active. Later, when you open your eyes, your inner mind will know that you no longer have to overeat and you no longer have to be hungry because, when you think of something to eat and it isn't mealtime, then your mind immediately reminds you of something better, more enjoyable, that you can just as easily do. It can be whatever you wish, something that really satisfies you.

You can enjoy whatever you do, even if it is by yourself. You can find yourself enjoyable. You can find yourself good company. You can find yourself fun to be with. As you tune in to yourself, you can understand yourself, you can love yourself. You can have a positive conversation with yourself, laugh and joke with yourself. Sing and dance with yourself. The more you learn to love yourself, the easier it becomes to develop positive change in your life.

You are developing a new attitude, for you are what you think; and all that you are thinking, you are becoming. Think how happy you are as you become more slim, more healthy every day. You have developed a slim life style. Other people are telling you how good you look. And you really enjoy preparing your food with love and a positive attitude.

(Complete your tape with the wake-up procedure.)

18   CIGARETTE CESSATION

Self-hypnosis is an effective and permanent way to eliminate the cigarette habit. Using this cycle to quit smoking reduces withdrawal and nervousness dramatically. You can maintain your present weight because you will not compensate for it by overeating. Your lungs will thank you. Your heart and circulatory system will thank you. Your breath will be fresher. You will feel healthier, more confident, and a lot happier. Most of all, your friends and loved ones will appreciate the change and thank you.

If all this sounds too good to be true, then try it. Conscientiously work with this cycle, then notice the results. As a side benefit, think of all the money you'll save on cigarettes and mouthwash.

Cigarette Cessation Cycle

(Continue your tape here.)

Like a skilled physician, my mind knows the exact remedies I need for a totally healthful way of life. My subconscious mind possesses an inner self-correcting system that is activating right now to realign past patterns and reshape my future. By choosing and developing healthful goals and through clear thinking, I begin a new life, setting new objectives and, with amazing momentum, moving in these directions.

I am starting a new life, determined to live each day fully to the utmost of my ability. I have new health and strength and energy to live fully and enjoy everything around me. I feel better and breathe easier. Friends notice the difference and tell me that I look better.

If there are signs of tension, I can relax by taking a deep breath and repeating these words in my mind: "I am relaxed. I am in complete control." I feel better every day because I am living in a new way, with full health and full enjoyment. Each and every day I am doing my best to fulfill my ideals and the purposes of my life, fulfilling them for myself and for everyone I love.

As I live fully, smoking becomes less and less a concern. If I think of cigarettes or if someone offers me one, or if I smell the smoke or there is any association with them, I will hear clearly in the back of my mind: "Stop!" I will hear it very strong. It will echo in my mind, "Stop," and I will take a deep breath.

My subconscious mind has far more resources than my conscious mind realizes. My body is now neutralizing the chemicals of the smoke. Even if I try to have a cigarette, my body may reject it. If someone tries to offer me a cigarette, I answer simply, "No, thank you."

If I happen to be around people smoking and the smoke annoys me, I put up a mental plexiglass screen to shield myself. In this way, others' smoke does not bother me or upset my health and well-being. In my mind I hear the words, "I am calm, I am relaxed."

Now I breathe easier and my breath is fresher. I am a clean air person, and I feel new strength and health and vitality. I find new creative outlets for my time and energy—perhaps a hobby or walking in nature or running—whatever I *enjoy* doing.

In my creative imagination I visualize a huge blackboard upon which I see the word "cigarettes." I now go to this blackboard and, as I erase that word, I erase, cancel and completely wipe away cigarettes from my life. I have eliminated the need or desire to smoke. (Pause) Now I have a clean slate. I return to the blackboard, pick up the chalk, and in place of the word "cigarettes" I write in capital letters the word "SUCCESS."

The right image comes to my mind as I create a positive symbol, an emblem of my success. I plant a new message in my inner mind, filling it with positive emotion and strength. My goal-image can be whatever I want it to be, and I bring my goals and ideals together into this vivid symbol. (Pause)

In a little while when my eyes open, I will be wide awake and comfortable. When I get up from my chair, I will know the joy and vitality of being a non-smoker and enjoy the feeling of feeling better. My lungs have already started rebuilding.

I mentally progress myself forward in time, imagining myself ahead into time—days, weeks, months, and years. What a wonderful feeling of accomplishment. It is accomplished—there was no withdrawal, no nervousness nor anxiety. I walk more, breathe better, and feel healthier. I did a great job—it's *already* accomplished.

(Complete your tape with the wake-up procedure.)

19 OVERCOMING INSOMNIA

Hypnosis is a safe, effective, and drug-free way of overcoming insomnia and of becoming a sound sleeper.

Most people suffering from insomnia have trouble "switching off" their minds after an active day. Instead of relaxing at bedtime, they replay the day's events in their minds, reliving the excitement or the frustration. Eventually they doze off, but by the time they get to sleep a sizable chunk of valuable sleep time has been wasted worrying.

Sleep and dream research gives new insight into this previously little-understood area of human experience. During sleep the conscious mind is temporarily resting, while the unconscious mind assumes control. Many psychic dreams and experiences take place during the sleep state. This is also a very creative time for artists, writers, and inventors.

During the sleep state there is mental and physical restoration, and in deep sleep emotional and physical self-healing occur. Restful, healing sleep is not only desirable to your well-being; it is vital. Of all the drug-free methods for overcoming insomnia, *Progressive Relaxation* is the most tested and effective.

Progressive Relaxation is as simple as systematically relaxing all the different parts of the body. There is a story about a man who had trouble sleeping. He went to his doctor who told him to lie down at night and say, "Toes go to sleep, ankles go to sleep, legs go to sleep, etc." That evening the man went to bed and tried it. He said, "Toes go to sleep, ankles go to sleep, legs go to sleep. . ." But then the man's wife came to bed in a new flowing negligée and the man said, "Everybody up! Wake up, everyone!" For this reason, do this cycle when you're *really* ready to sleep.

Time the pace of this cycle slowly. It is most effective when delivered in a low, measured, and somewhat monotonous voice.

Overcoming Insomnia Cycle

(Continue your tape here.)

If you allow yourself to become completely relaxed,
there will be no tense muscles anywhere in your body.
If there is any discomfort, let it go.
You can let it completely dissolve,
like a spoonful of sugar in a cup of hot tea.

You can adjust your breathing to a slow,
comfortable pace.
You can visualize the different parts of your body
relaxing and going to sleep.
If your attention drifts to your toes,
they will become pleasantly relaxed.
You may be aware of the warm circulation in them.

If you send relaxation to your feet. . .
the soles of your feet. . .the instep. . .the ankles. . .
they may feel the warm circulation also.
You may feel a gentle, warm, soothing sensation.
You may feel the same soothing process
flowing up through your calves. . .your shins. . .
gently relaxing the knees.

As the knees relax, you may feel the relaxation
going to your upper legs.
Allow gentle, relaxing waves to calm the buttocks. . .
abdomen. . .stomach.
You can relax the small of the lower back. . .the spine. . .

Allow the heart to settle into a slow, easy, rhythmic beat.
If you breathe out, the chest will relax;
your breathing can come slow, relaxed.
You can allow the fingers to relax. . .the hands. . .
the wrists. . .
You may feel the relaxing warmth moving into the
forearm. . .the upper arm. . .the shoulders.
If you relax the neck, all the muscles will become loose
and limber.

Allow the jaw to relax and perhaps fall a little.
The relaxing feeling can go to the cheeks and the eyes. . .
around the eyes.
The face can become serene and relaxed. . .
the forehead. Let go.

Form a soothing symbol that means
rest and quiet for you.
You may visualize a gentle, permeating light,
filtering softly throughout your body,
or you may feel your entire body floating safely
in a vast, infinite, shoreless sea of pure, clear warmth.
This is a time of quiet, restful healing and gentle dreams.
Time melts and flows softly.
Enjoy peace of mind as you allow yourself to wander.
Calm your mind as you have calmed your body.
You have established a pattern for healthy sleep.
As you breathe slowly a drifting can occur. . .

*(Complete this cycle with the suggestions for "Going into
Nighttime Sleep.")*

20   PREPARING FOR SURGERY

If you have faced surgery, you already know that feeling of panic which results. You may have known people who had difficult or painful times in the hospital and heard frightening stories. Just not knowing for sure what to expect can cause anxiety. Self-hypnosis can help take the trauma out of this very frightening experience. With preliminary programing, the subconscious can be prepared.

The woman who originally drafted this cycle faced such feelings. She had had two very difficult and painful surgeries, and felt unable to face a third. She took her first self-hypnosis course in order to work specifically on this problem. Only then was she able to overcome and deal with her fears. She was so successful with her major operation and speedy recovery that the doctors were amazed and were talking about it long afterward. Complications which could easily have manifested didn't, and she had very little pain. She felt like a new woman upon opening her eyes and continues to feel the same way.

Preparing for Surgery Cycle

(Continue your tape here.)

Sometimes I consciously hope and pray for the things I
want in life,
and sometimes I allow my subconscious mind to
automatically accomplish things for me.
As an example, I enjoy being alive.
To live, I need oxygen;
to get oxygen, I must breathe.
I can pay attention to each breath consciously,
if I so decide,
or I can allow my subconscious to do this automatically.

In this relaxed state,
I am discovering that there are many more things
available than I have ever dreamed of.
I feel a desire to allow my subconscious mind to help me
at this important time of my life.
I perceive that my subconscious may already
be helping me without my conscious awareness,
and what happens at a subconscious level is often
more real,
more automatic,
and life-sustaining,
if I simply allow it to help me.

No matter what any person believes,
no matter what I consciously believe,
the important thing is
that my subconscious mind is working for me
and for my successful operation.
The subconscious mind can view reality
through a different sense of time.
I can, for example, review a happy scene from my
childhood as if it were almost happening right now.
It is easy to take a few moments and relive it.
(Pause)
I can also condense time
or expand time.

I can also look ahead in time
and, looking ahead,
imagine that it has already happened.
I can look at anything I wish
and see it clearly.
I can see myself having already gone into this surgery.
My operation was successful in every way.
My doctors and anesthesiologist automatically did the
right things at the right time,
and it all worked out fine.

Throughout the experience I was calm,
peaceful, and confident.
Some people afterward said that I was "cheerful."
I slept comfortably and peacefully
because I already knew how to calm my mind
and put it on "automatic pilot."
And even though I may have been unconscious,
my subconscious mind responded to my body's needs
and acted upon them correctly.

After the operation, the nurses made me feel safe,
comfortable, and secure.
I got plenty of rest and enjoyed
the visits of family and friends.
Total recovery was such a positive experience.

I am as a new person,
refreshed, and heading for a healthy new future.
Back home now with this very happy memory,
I will look back next year and the year after that
and say, "Thank God that it was all so easy."

I feel pleased in realizing
that my subconscious did a great job,
that I did a great job.
Now it isn't really important for me to remember
all that I accomplished here today;
my subconscious mind understands it
and, at the proper time, acts upon it.
The information has been processed.
I need not consciously know today

that I experienced an "overview" of time
and that I was perhaps completely anesthetized.

I realize that I am the author
of my success.
And soon, when I awaken,
I may feel as if I were
just waiting to begin.

(Complete your tape with the wake-up procedure.)

21   ATTRACTIVE FINGERNAILS

This is the cycle that cultivates the inner mind to help
you stop nail-biting. Perhaps you have tried mustering
up all your reserves of willpower and forcing your hands
into your pockets—now there is a better and easier way.

If you have had enough of torn and jagged fingernails, now is the time to do something about it. You may
wish to carry a fingernail file in your pocket or purse during the month you are using this cycle. This way you can
smooth the rough edges when your fingernails begin to
grow again.

Attractive Fingernails Cycle

(Continue your tape here.)

Imagine yourself in the future—progressing through
time, moving into time and through time. . .
and visualize your hands. . .
not as they *used* to be, but as they are *becoming,*
as they *are.*
Create a vivid image of your fingernails as smooth,
attractive (good-looking), and feeling good.
Look at them, touch them.
Enjoy the way they look and feel.
Your mind creates your own reality.
And, as your mind is creating this reality for you. . .
this is how your hands got better. . .

Long ago, you reached a decision, you made up your mind
to the fact that you would like to do something better
than bite your nails.

Nobody wants to chew on parts of the body,
and you don't have to do anything you don't like.

Your mind is not a computer, but the human mind
functions like a computer in many ways.
Over the course of time, certain responses
get programmed into it.
Now your mind
is programing in
another response. . .
a better way of doing things.
Whenever it seems you want to bite your nails,
your hand will move toward your face,
but you can let it stop
before it reaches your mouth.

And you will look at your hand—
while you decide deliberately—
whether you really want to bite your nails.
If you decide that you do, then go ahead and chew them.
But, of course, nobody really wants to chew
on parts of (his/her) own body.
So you will decide that you would rather
leave your nails alone,
and you can let your hand move easily away from
your face.
And, as you do this, you can remind yourself
of how attractive (good-looking) your hands are
getting each day.

Day by day, they become more and more attractive.
And you become prouder of them as each day passes.

Now, let your mind rehearse this reality for you.
Imagine that your hand is moving toward your face. . .
without even thinking of it. . .
now watch your hand stop.
Really. . .watch your hand stop.

You're looking at it. . .
deciding what you want to do with it.
Now, let your hand move away. . .
while you remember how attractive your hands
are becoming.
Each time you do this your programing becomes
stronger.
And in time. . .any time you choose. . .
it will be second nature, and you will remind yourself
that you have something better to do with your hands.
Something that you choose, the right image, will come
to you.
Create a vivid goal-image, a symbol of something you
really want to do. (Pause)
And see it already accomplished, a positive end result,
and you are pleased and thankful for your success.

(Complete your tape with the wake-up procedure.)

22   CHILDBIRTHING

A positive attitude, quiet meditation, and excellent nutrition are the foundations of a healthy pregnancy. Many couples are now taking classes together so that both partners can share in the birthing adventure. If you are learning techniques on a physical level, you can also work together on a mental, emotional, and spiritual level.

The trend today is toward active participation of the father, not only as a coach at the birth but beforehand with positive preparatory suggestions. This cycle can be read verbatim or it can be spoken in the spontaneous, loving words of the father. It is as much a silent suggestion for the child as a gentle reassurance for the mother. The Cayce readings state:

> Here is something that each and every mother should know. The manner in which the attitude is kept has much to do with the character of the soul that would choose to enter through those channels [of birth] at the particular period.   2803-6

Childbirthing Cycle

(Continue your tape here.)

New life is forming, growing, and moving within you.
You are part of the promise and the destiny of life itself.
A very important event is going to take place in your life,
a normal, biological function.
You're going to have a baby.
What is happening now is a process of freeing
the kicking, moving being
who's been a part of your body for so long.
Soon it will be time for the baby to become its own
separate person.
One cycle is ending and, immediately, another is
beginning.

What has been called "labor" is the inbetween condition,
the fulcrum,
the small time and space between two worlds.
Change from one stage to another brings pressure,
and then release.
You will soon experience this also
as the change is completed and fulfilled.
You can feel this and embrace it
and welcome it as refreshing and totally natural.
With mind, you build a healthy attitude
and happy expectation.
Happy childbirthing has much to do with a healthy
viewpoint.
It is something remarkably beautiful.
Being a channel of new life is said to be a holy experience.
With this understanding and proper breathing,
possible discomfort is lessened.

Later, as you begin labor,
meditate on the tremendous universal force—
the life force—
you are participating with.
Whenever you feel your body tightening up,
actively think "release," "let go."
There is a time for contraction

and a time for letting go.
Release, and welcome the process.
You are learning to relax,
flow, melt with the rhythm of life itself.
With patience and positive expectation,
all things are possible.

Happily picture yourself at an ocean beach.
Watch the endless waves rushing to the shore—
the ebb and flow of the sea.
Observe it advancing and withdrawing over the sand.
Become part of it; flowing into it,
you become part of the rhythm of your own body,
the tightening and releasing,
the breathing in and breathing out,
giving birth to your baby.

With appropriate physical and mental exercises,
you are preparing yourself for this day of days.
As you get into the rhythm and are working with your
mind and body,
the easier and smoother it becomes.
Breathe as you've practiced in classes or read about.
Each time you breathe in, breathe in "rest."
Each time you breathe out, willfully breathe out
any stress.
Shift your focus away from the pressure
to think of the final pleasure.

Mentally and emotionally feel yourself
joyfully, totally aware, and participating.
See it as already accomplished.
Listen to that first sound of new life.
Create a vivid symbol of bonding.
(Pause)

You knew you could do it, and you did.
You did well and it was wonderful.
It is a healthy, beautiful child.
Remember to savor each precious moment.
Relax and flow with your body's natural rhythm.

After all, your body knows what it's doing.
Just relax and let it do its job.
Stand back in joy and amazement and
watch the continuing mystery of creation unfold.
The life force is now in you and with you.

(Complete your tape with the wake-up procedure.)

23 WART ELIMINATION

Probably everyone has heard of some strange and un-usual way to remove warts. Treatment of warts in the Cayce readings ranges from hypnosis and suggestion to the electric needle. Most common of all applications was the use of baking soda mixed with castor oil. This can be applied with a Band-Aid and left in place overnight.

Even with self-hypnosis there are many approaches to work with. A holistic strategy may be to "befriend" the wart—hear what it has to say—and then allow it to de-part. Of course, you can use *your own* suggestion along *with* a physical remedy at the same time.

The approach in this cycle* may seem a bit drastic at first—cutting the wart off from its life support—but warts do not become malignant and appear to serve no useful function. People have had excellent results with this method, and it is definitely more pleasant than an electric needle.

Note: This method and variations on it have been listed in a number of science books; it is drastic, but acceptable.

Wart Elimination Cycle

(Continue your tape here.)

It is important for you to learn some things
about yourself.
You can learn that the flow of blood to the cells
carries oxygen and nutrients to each cell,
helping them to grow and multiply,

to create new cells,
to speed whatever healing must be done.
And the most wonderful thing about this process
is that you can learn to control it.
This is something you can easily understand
and begin to learn to do
as you become aware of your physical body
in a new and positive way.
Healing can take place at any time.
(Pause)

You can visualize the structure of a wart.
You can see that it is useless and unnecessary.
See the network of tiny veins and blood vessels that
bring it nourishment.
And now you can discover that,
by closing off the veins and capillaries
that feed it,
you can deprive each wart of nourishment and nutrients.
It receives no warmth, no attention,
and begins to starve.
And, in time, it shrinks; then vanishes,
so that healthy new tissue can form in its place.
Feel a sense of pride about yourself,
your body, and the healing process.
(Pause)

Take a deep breath now
and think of healthy, pink new skin.
As you let the breath out slowly,
become aware of this new skin.
Is it especially sensitive?
Does it feel cool?
Warm?

Beneath the skin are many veins and capillaries
that carry blood and nourishment and warmth
throughout your body—especially your (a localized area
may be inserted; i.e., face, hands, feet, etc.).
As you become aware of this, it is possible
for you to actually feel the warmth,

the blood vessels expanding to pump even more
nourishment and oxygen through your skin.
You can become aware of this
and experience it in whatever way you wish.
Perhaps you might recognize it
as a pleasant tingling
or a kind of soothing warmth.
Now allow that warmth to fill you and experience
new feelings in your body.
You are learning a new awareness of yourself.
You are discovering how to appreciate yourself,
to accept yourself.
And with this acceptance—the warmth and the
attention—you feel more confident, more comfortable,
more at ease, and pleased with yourself.
Imagine yourself as you *can* look—
not just one part, but your whole body.
With a pleasant sense of awareness
and a positive mental attitude,
you experience warmth and healing energy.

Does the new skin feel tight
or slightly tender?
Notice the tissue underneath the skin.
Can you feel the blood vessels pulsing
as they carry nutrients to the cells?
(Pause)

Imagine that you are resting on a secluded beach;
really picture yourself at that beach
under a bright sun
shining on your entire body, especially on your
(hand, feet, etc.)
—a hot sun, getting hotter,
with the heat penetrating your skin;
a good feeling of heat that warms you completely
with a soothing, penetrating warmth
that brings healing;
feeling warmth,
with possibly a slight tenderness,
as healthy new cells combine,

pink skin forms, and the healing takes place.
Now that your inner mind has recorded it,
it is something you can experience
at any time you wish.
You can create this same feeling
by simply slowing your breathing
and visualizing the healing—thankful that
it is already being accomplished.

(Complete your tape with the wake-up procedure.)

CHAPTER TEN

Cycles for Touching a Larger Consciousness

24 ATTRACTING LOVE

The sages of all time have known that love is life's greatest blessing. Everyone wants and needs love. We all need others; we need the emotional and spiritual nourishment of human relationships. Human comfort is a natural remedy for stress, tension, and doubt. Loving, touching, and sharing are normal, healthy expressions of the human adventure.

Fear—of the unknown, of rejection, of the loss of love, of criticism—is a major cause of loneliness. Sadly, this very fear can create a vicious cycle of anger, boredom, or depression which, in turn, creates more fear and isolation. Loneliness is a state of mind, and the solution to it is to build bridges instead of walls.

You may have goals to be more loving, but lack of knowledge of how to achieve them. Self-hypnosis can be an effective tool for opening your heart by changing the way you look at yourself and teaching respectful communication with your inner mind. In the best-seller *Living, Loving and Learning,* Dr. Leo Buscaglia writes, "If you don't like the scene you're in, if you're unhappy, if you're lonely, if you don't feel that things are happening, change your scene. Paint a new backdrop. Surround yourself with new actors. Write a new play—and if it's not a good play, get to hell off the stage and write another. There are millions of plays—as many as there are people." (Ballantine Books, 1982, p. 53)

Learning to love yourself in healthy ways is the first step toward loving others. Seeing the beauty in yourself is as necessary as seeing the beauty in others. You can attract love by creating an atmosphere of love in your life. Your thoughts determine whom you attract into your world. This cycle can help bring more friendship, love, and beauty into your daily experience.

Attracting Love Cycle

(Continue your tape here.)

In *The Prophet* Kahlil Gibran said, "And think not that you can direct the course of love, for love, if it finds you worthy, directs your course."

Truly, I can prepare for love by becoming worthy of love. And the best way to prepare for love is simply to start loving. I can learn to love myself and to love others, for love is life's greatest blessing.

I realize, no matter what I once believed, that my belief in being worthy of love is all that really matters. My reality is a life of giving and receiving love, and my inner mind is creating and realizing this happy reality.

I am learning to be at peace with myself for this is the first step to being happy with others. I am beginning to see more of the joy and beauty of life that is surrounding me daily.

I am preparing for love by speaking kindly to all I meet. I am consciously looking for the good and the positive in everyone. I tell people of their fine points, their gentle qualities. I listen carefully to the words that others speak.

I am attracting love by being considerate in my thoughts, my words, and my actions. I am building bridges that span the gulf that may once have separated me from others, and change builds from my heart as well as my mind.

I am learning what I need and want from a relationship. And I am also learning what I can and will give to this relationship, to this someone special. I trust that this person is as anxious to meet me as I am to meet (him/her). I will not prejudge this person but appreciate (him/her), as the person (he/she) *already* is.

We are going and growing *toward* each other, and soon our paths will meet. I trust that I am becoming worthy of love because I can begin to feel the joy and the lightness, the spontaneous laughter, that comes with love. I realize that love is more than verbally saying, "I love you." It is saying it with my daily actions, the things I do.

In the past I may have thought that happiness would come only after I found my ideal lover. This old attitude limited my personal growth, so I am deciding to be truly happy right *now,* today. And because my sincere joy makes me more attractive, this helps my lover to recognize me even more quickly.

In my creative imagination I can picture a positive union. I am visualizing a vivid symbol of fulfilling love. I bring my goals and ideals together, plant a new image, and nurture it with positive emotion. (Pause)

At an inner level of my mind, I realize that this has already happened, that we are already together. The beloved and I are already one, for love—like mind—is ageless. It reaches beyond time and space. I am feeling the days, months, and years of warm and tender embrace. Waves of response fill my life with physical, mental, emotional and spiritual fulfillment.

(Complete your tape with the wake-up procedure.)

25   DEVELOPING PSYCHIC ABILITY

Everyone has ESP (extrasensory perception); everyone has psychic potential, but many people are not aware of their inner gifts. The Edgar Cayce readings say, ". . .the psychic forces, the psychic faculties, lie dormant or active in every individual, and await only that awakening or arousing, or the developing under those environs that make for the accentuation of same in the individual." (5752-1)

Some people are aware of their psychic gifts but don't know how to fine-tune them; others know how to fine-tune their gifts but don't know how to apply them. Although there are no shortcuts to psychic development, this cycle can help you do all three: discover your personal abilities, fine-tune them, and apply these talents to help yourself and others. Your psychic ability can be enhanced and accentuated by patiently working with this cycle.

Psychic development is also letting go of the fear of the unknown and building toward your ideals. The readings say, "Thus ye may constructively use that ability of spiritual attunement, which is the birthright of each soul; ye may use it as a helpful influence in experiences in the earth." (2475-1) Training the psychic within you is expanding the frontiers of your mind and slowly opening yourself to new spiritual realms of life.

Your latent psychic gifts—your hidden human reserves—can be awakened. They may be the result of work already accomplished in other times and places. These gifts of the spirit can be best brought out by living and thinking unselfishly and by loving unconditionally. Your achievements are a direct result of your loving thoughts directed at helping yourself and sharing with others.

Developing Psychic Ability Cycle

(Continue your tape here.)

If you take a deep breath and exhale it very slowly, you can imagine that your breath is like the ocean with the waves coming and going. Perhaps you can hear the music of the waves upon the shore. Watch the waves as you breathe in and breathe out. Imagine that you are lying down, resting upon the shore. You can imagine all the weight leaving your body. Use your imagination, for it is a profound gift to use and enjoy.

Just imagine yourself beginning to float—safely—bit by bit. Allow yourself to float comfortably a little bit above where you are lying. Enjoy yourself rising up and floating in the air.

If you take another breath, you can release pressure and tension that once held you down. And releasing them, you begin to rise a little more—safely and pleasantly.

You may imagine yourself as a seagull or an eagle or a dove. Perhaps you are sailing with a hang glider or a helium balloon—the right image will come to you. Rise up on the wings of your mind. Feel yourself soaring, gliding, climbing upward to your higher self. Floating freely in the air, you can observe the world unfolding below you. See the colors of the planet: the blues and greens, the earth tones.

Sense the majesty of the heavens and the panorama of the living universe. Soar and glide to the rhythm of life. Ride the wind and soar higher, higher. You have freed yourself from the earthly bonds that once shackled your mind to convention, self-doubt, and confusion. Feel the quiet radiance of life surrounding you, hear the harmony that is you in tune with creation. Be still and observe and know.

Glide upward, ever upward, toward understanding, toward light, and toward beauty. Beauty surrounds you in this sanctity of space. Here is where other worlds exist beyond the confines of your everyday mind. And just as a seed contains the promise of fulfillment, so does your mind already contain the promise of greater gifts.

If you choose a path of service to others, you can discover and develop your inner psychic gifts. When you choose to serve others with patience, love, and compassion, you automatically become a channel of blessings. Be aware and alert as the spirit of truth beckons you to new understanding, new directions, and new dimensions. When spirit beckons, follow!— carrying a prayer in your mind and in your heart.

As you let go of old fixed ideas, doubts, and other negative influences, you open the way for new love, patience, and gentleness. The spirit guides you to enjoy the rewards of your new reality. Higher knowledge is usually communicated in silence, so you may choose to go daily into the greater silence within.

Be receptive to the guidance of your universal mind. Your higher mind guides you and protects you, even when you are not consciously aware of it. Grow in the silence of your spiritual self.

Be still and listen. Your higher mind already knows your needs and guides you to live a clear new way each day. Your universal mind guides you to action by giving you gifts of the spirit. I Corinthians says, ". . .the manifestation of the Spirit is given to every man [or woman] to profit withal.
For to one is given by the Spirit the word of wisdom;
To another the word of knowledge by the same Spirit;
To another faith by the same Spirit;

To another the gifts of healing. . .
To another the working of miracles;
to another prophecy;
to another discerning of spirits;
to another divers kinds of tongues;
to another the interpretation of tongues;
But all these worketh that one and the selfsame Spirit,
dividing to every [person] severally as he will."
(I Corinthians 12:7-11)

Some people are given more than one psychic gift. You
may already have developed several gifts. It is good to
apply your gifts and not "to put them under a bushel."
Gifts of the spirit can be used often as in
Romans 12:6:

"Having then gifts differing according to the grace
that is given to us, whether prophecy, let us
prophesy. . ." Open wide the door of spirit and rightly use
the creative energy that is within you.

One way to determine which are your special intuitive
gifts is to try each of them. When you talk with
someone, listen—really listen—with your inner ear as
well as your outer ears. You may hear things being
said at the inner level that are not spoken at the outer
levels. Listen also to your inner voice and respond
to it.

When you see a person or an event, look—really look—
and perceive it with your inner vision. See and
understand the workings behind the scenes. Open
yourself to all the impressions; look deeper than the
surface. If you feel that you may have a gift of
healing, use this gift. If you feel that you may have a
gift of tongues, use this gift. If you have a gift of
prophecy, use this gift to serve others, with their
cooperation. Be thankful and use your gifts daily.

Look into the deep recesses of your mind and awaken
the silent dreamer. In the inner recesses of your own
mind rests all knowledge and ability. The permanent
records of life are kept of every act and deed, of all

history and all thought, of all medicine and technology, and of all advancements. They are kept in your own consciousness and, as you look deep within, you will see all that exists, that has existed, and will exist. This is already in the recesses of your own mind, your soul-mind. And as you are willing to accept yourself and as you look deep within, then you see and understand and perceive this; and grow and build toward the light. (Pause)

Now create a picture or vivid symbol of yourself using and applying your gifts of the spirit. Bring your accomplished ideals and goals together into a specific image, and visualize it as already accomplished. (Pause)

Now you can slowly return from your upward flight— returning as a floating feather, circling gently, and landing softly back on the beach. Bringing back something positive and helpful with you. Hear the waves and recall the thoughts, feelings, symbols, and ideas from your journey. You are developing your gifts and learning to use them daily, as you open wide to the new spiritual age that is before you.

(Complete your tape with the wake-up procedure.)

26   CHILD MEDITATION

This cycle is designed to be played for children at bedtime, just before they go to sleep, and can be especially helpful to them during times of anxiety. It contains easier words and simpler symbols than the adult cycles, but many of those cycles can be adapted to fit your child's needs as well. Depending on the age of your child, you may wish to simplify the wording of this cycle or design a more personal cycle.

This meditation cycle is self-contained; i.e., it is complete in itself. It begins with a guided meditation, followed by positive suggestions and a special white-light visualization cycle, and finishes with suggestions to drift into regular nighttime sleep afterward. The cycle explores and discusses the spiritual centers in the physical body. (These centers are also called chakras and relate to the body's endocrine system.)

This cycle is specifically designed to develop young people's imaginations by having them visualize on nature and their own internal beings. The Cayce readings recommend: "Then, as the development of the mind of the child, develop its imaginative forces...Acquaint such a mind with the activities in nature..." (5747-1)

While in his trance state, Edgar Cayce gave numerous readings for young people. He said that the hope of the world rested upon the developing minds of the younger generation. For some children, he recommended hypnosis or suggestive therapeutics to help them with certain problems. Their parents can give positive suggestions at bedtime as a method for healing, help, and guidance.

Edgar Cayce outlined a simple and clear procedure. First, he recommended that the *parent* give the suggestions and not relegate this job to a babysitter. Second, the suggestions should always be positive, telling the child *what to do*. With bed-wetting, for example, tell the child that he or she will awaken when the need arises, and will get up and relieve the body. Do not say, "Don't wet the bed." Instead say, "You will get up and go take care of the need." Third, suggestions are best given in a loving manner at bedtime, while the child is drifting off into sleep. This is the mind's most receptive time.

In a personal reading for a young girl, Mr. Cayce explained it this way:

> Then as the body goes to sleep, sit by same [her], make those positive suggestions in this form—this is a suggestion, though it may be altered at times to add that which is the heart-felt wish of the mother...
>
> 1104-2

In another personal reading for a very young boy the readings stated:

. . .let the parents, in meditation over and with the
body as it begins its slumber, give these:

Not merely as words but in their *own* words. . .

1314-2

Child Meditation Cycle

(This cycle is complete and all-inclusive.)

You can keep your eyes open for a minute and sort of
look upward, but you don't have to look at anything
special. I will count downward from ten to one and
you can just blink your eyes slowly—like in slow
motion—with every number. Ten. . .nine. . .eight. . .
seven. . .six. . .five. . .four. . .three. . .two. . .and one.
Now you can close your eyes and keep them closed
and I will tell you why we did that.

That was just to relax your eyelids. And right now, in
your eyelids, you might notice a tired feeling, a
pleasant feeling or a sort of comfortable, heavy
feeling. You can pretend that this heavy or tired
feeling is spreading out and going to other parts of
your body. See if you can imagine the feeling going to
your face and your head. . .to your arms and hands. . .
to your chest and your back. . .then down to your legs
and feet. . .even all the way out to the tips of your
toes.

And soon you may begin to feel heavy or light, but
heavy or light in a nice way. This is what being
relaxed means. You don't have to do anything. You
can hear my voice, but you don't really have to listen
to it. You can hear my voice, but at the same time you
could be doing other things, like listening to music or
looking at colors or quietly playing in your mind. It
really doesn't matter.

You might find yourself drifting or you might hear all
that I say. You can imagine yourself going to play
safely near the ocean or a lake or even a pool. Perhaps

it is a nice warm day, but not too hot because there are a few clouds in the sky. If you are playing in the sand, you may notice that it gets cooler as you dig down, and the more you dig down, the cooler it all gets.

If there are friends around, you may wish to splash in the water. You can have fun splashing and playing. The air smells nice and fresh. Maybe you feel *so* good that you want to tell your friends just how good you feel. It is good just to be alive, just to be you.

As you play in the water or run on the sand, you can meet other friends and talk with them also. Maybe they will walk with you and talk with you at the same time. The warm sand feels good on your feet. And even though you are having a great time, you may want to lie down on the beach and rest awhile.

If you take a deep breath, you can feel very quiet. Maybe you can begin to go exploring with a flashlight. A special flashlight that shines anywhere and you can imagine that light in your head and let it shine inside of you. This light shows the place of your dreams and it gives you spiritual strength.

Right near this place you can shine your special white light flashlight to another place in your head also, but this new place is your intuition. That means that this is the place where you can know things without anybody telling you. You can keep your nice special secrets here also; this is a comfortable and warm place.

Now you can picture more light—a beautiful clear white light, and you can put it in your neck and throat area. This is a special place for rest and tranquility. You may get good ideas or inspiration from this place also.

Now you can bring your special flashlight and shine it in your heart area. Make your light shine real bright, for this is a special place of harmony and balance and love.

Now bring your light—your clear white light—into your stomach area. This is the place of wisdom and creativity; here is energy and zest for life.

Continue down, bringing your special light to below your stomach. And let your light shine bright, for this is the seat of your soul. Here is a place of spiritual awakening.

And now, where your legs meet your body, you can shine your light. This is the place of new life, and a special place of physical strength and stamina.

And now, shine your white light all around your entire body, splash your body with wonderful light. And you shine with the light that is within you. This special light can help you and heal you and encourage you to grow happy and joyful.

There are many blessings surrounding you. You can say to yourself, "I am so very thankful." And being thankful helps you to feel good. And feeling good can help you have nice dreams. And in a little while, when you gently drift into your night's sleep, you can have good dreams, happy dreams. And tomorrow bring back something good, something special from your dreams.

And tomorrow, when you awaken, you can feel good and say, "I had a wonderful sleep." You are resting your body, your mind, and your spirit. You may already be drifting into quiet, gentle sleep. You can go at your own pace. You are growing each day and you are safe and we love you very much.

(If you are playing background music, allow the music to continue playing softly for a few minutes.)

27 BEYOND TOMORROW

This cycle can help you look forward in time. Future

time progression, or prophecy, is a natural gift for some people, but it may be developed by almost everyone with the help of this cycle.

Whether you are reflecting on a distant past or gazing into a hazy future, openmindness is vital. Be prepared to disregard any former prejudices. Have patience and try to dismiss an impression of tomorrow because it does not fit any of your preconceived notions. The future is but a subtle series of insights, possibilities, and probabilities. Although the past has congealed, the future is still fluid and forming.

Future exploration, time travel, using this cycle can be a unique and exciting adventure.

Beyond Tomorrow Cycle

(Continue your tape here.)

Be aware of a soft, radiant, white light filtering through your mind. Just become aware now of your consciousness being aware of itself. . .as in a dream within a dream. . .looking into a mirror of time. . . flowing into timeless time.

Feel your entire body floating in a vast, infinite, shoreless sea of glowing white light, an essence so light and luminous that it's like a shining mist. See and feel this gentle, illuminating force. It is your own consciousness and it is linked to universal consciousness.

As you feel this warm energy softly bathing every atom and cell of your being, be aware that you are an eternal spiritual being who uses the mind, emotions, and body as instruments of your will. You have the ability to choose whatever thoughts, emotions, feelings and sensations you direct your awareness to. And in this ability is your free will as an eternal spiritual being.

Now you are becoming more and more aware of your freedom to go beyond the limits of the physical body. You can progress yourself anywhere in space and time by simply directing your attention there. Time, calendar, and space may be illusions of material limitations in respect to the five senses. Time and calendar are inconsequential in the thoughts and vibratory or outer dimensional forces of your eternal self. As you look within and listen to your inner voice, your intuitive pathways will open to new vision and insight.

You belong to that infinite essence which is beyond time and space, because there is only the eternal now as it exists on each level of experience. In the realm of higher consciousness, everything that has ever existed and everything that can ever exist on the physical, emotional or mental levels exists now as a possibility. And you have the complete ability to see and hear and experience all these things and to know them and to understand them for what they are. The answers are already deep within you.

With patience you can move through space and time to become aware of events that may be waiting to happen. Allow yourself to go, and feel yourself safely and comfortably going into time—through time—beyond time—above time—to those events which are waiting to be experienced and understood. Your inner mind knows far more than you think it knows. Be intimate with your own mind and, reaching the inner self, venture deep, deep into the gentle recesses of your mind—to a place you have never touched before. This is the storehouse of full knowledge in the still waters of your soul. (Pause)

By opening your mind and trusting your inner impressions, you can move freely through time and space. You may be able to bring back with you insight and understanding that can help you in the present. You can mentally discuss and visually picture what you are doing and what is happening.

Look at what you are wearing in this place. Make a mental note of all that you see. What are you wearing on your feet? What are you hearing? Create vivid symbols and word-images to bring back with you. (Pause)

Now begin the slow and careful journey back through time—into what you call the present. And as you come back through the mist of time, you bring back something that will help you.

(Complete your tape with the wake-up procedure.)

28   SONG OF LIFE

This cycle was designed by a musician, who developed it for the purpose of helping you tune in to the sounds of your inner self. (Sounds from the inner ear are called clairaudience.) Every person has a personal vibration, an inner sound, which is as unique as fingerprints.

The author of this "Song of Life" cycle writes: "The most wonderful thing has begun to take place for me since we did this cycle and since I have made conscious efforts to 'retune' myself in general! You know how sometimes when you're by yourself in the house or at work or even around people you either whistle or hum a little tune?

"Well, oddly enough, as a musician, I don't do that; still too inhibited? But, whatever; what does happen now is that every once in awhile (and I make it happen more often now that I know what's going on), I will begin to hum—a single note—and so help me, as I do, that particular noise/sound literally sends a vibratory response throughout my entire body; the feeling is wondrous!

"I literally feel, sense, hear, and see my entire body pulling itself together. My circulation rushes around, my muscles 'tune up,' and my heart, mind, and soul feel like they will soar into the sky. I have learned that it is truly my own personal vibration and, when it happens, I feel that I have indeed become part of the Universal Sound."

This cycle is like learning a new step in the dance of life. If you play a musical instrument, you can record *your own* favorite music as background for this (or any other) tape.

The Edgar Cayce readings often spoke of the value of music. An eleven-year-old girl asked, "What course of studies should I pursue in secondary and higher education?" Her readings said:

> Music! History of, the activity of, all of those various forms. If you learn music, you'll learn history. If you learn music, you'll learn mathematics. If you learn music, you'll learn most all there is to learn—unless it's something bad.   3053-3

Another reading stated:

> Do learn music. It is part of the beauty of the spirit. For remember, music alone may span that space between the finite and the infinite. In the harmony of sound, the harmony of color, even the harmony of motion itself, its beauty [music] is all akin to that expression of the soul-self in the harmony of the mind, if used properly in relationship to body.   3659-1

Song of Life Cycle

(Continue your tape here.)

And now that you are in your favorite place of relaxation, surrounded by symbols of tranquility, you can slowly begin to listen to sounds within you.

Start with your mind and hear the sounds you know so well:
the sound of a finely tuned engine,
children playing in a school yard,
church bells ringing,
and the crickets singing.

And now, if you listen very closely,
you may hear plants as they grow.

Now, begin to come within your mind,
into your own body, and know that
it, too, produces the most beautiful of sounds.
Start right now to tune in to your very own
personal vibrations.
Begin by sensing the internal sound of your body;
begin by feeling the internal sound within you.
And now, hear deep within you
and throughout your entire body,
the slow tuning
of sound within your body.

The sound can enter through a light surrounding
the top of your head
and continue down through your face
and into your shoulders and arms.

And now the sound can touch your heart and lungs,
and you will feel so very happy
at the sounds you are hearing
and feeling within you.
And the sound continues
throughout your body, to your legs, down to your feet,
and circling back again through your body.

As you hear and feel the sound traveling throughout your
body, you can begin to unlock, within yourself,
the harmonic tones which create your whole vibration,
and let yourself guide the vibrations and combine them
into a single tone which is your own harmonic vibration.
Listen now, with your inner ear.
Let yourself hear and feel your own tone, the vibration
which is the creation of the song of your soul.
Hear it now within you;
let your new-found harmonics
hum within your body as they sing and rejoice.
Enjoy your own song of life.
And, as you continue to let your soul sing
its own vibrations within you,

expand and begin to seek an even greater attunement.
Reach out and hear with all your senses
the sound of the Universe.
Know and recognize the cosmic vibrations of this planet,
Earth, and beyond—into infinity.
It is one sound.
Hear it with your inner ear and feel the experience.
Enjoy this profound vibration. (Pause)

And the more aware you become of your own inner
harmony,
the more aware you become of the Universal Sound.
You can let yourself become one soul,
in tune with the Universe
and its song of life. (Pause)

Let yourself feel this great joy of soul sound,
your song of being alive.
And the more you feel and hear
this personal song of life you have created,
the more you will let yourself hear it each day.
Each day brings more harmony into your life.

Each day this powerful song of your soul,
your joy of living,
will touch you and, then,
reach out to other souls around you,
spreading a Universal Vibration, a Universal Sound.
It brings you into harmony with yourself and others.
(Pause)

Let yourself feel the great joy;
let yourself hear the vibrations of your soul song
and sing within yourself.
Flow with the dance and rhythm of life.
Dance to the song of your life.

(Complete your tape with the wake-up procedure.)

29 FRIENDS AND SOUL MATES

Have you ever met a stranger with whom you felt
you'd been acquainted before? Was there a certain famil-

iarity about him or her? Did you feel a rush of excitement, a flush, or a heat-wave? Did your heart skip a beat? Was there a knowing look in the stranger's eyes? Where had you met before? Was it perhaps someone you recognized from a distant time and place?

This is a very unusual cycle in that it is not "focused" on a specific goal like the others; it is more like a "stream of consciousness." This cycle was written by a woman who wished to help herself be more aware of the people coming into her life. It is offered only to demonstrate that cycles can serve a multitude of purposes and have purely personal meanings. For example, some people may create cycles from their favorite poems, short stories or essays like "Desiderata."

Use this unique cycle as a model for personal projects or as an aid to opening your awareness and recognizing people you knew from long ago and far away. You might possibly achieve understanding and insight into reasons for your meeting them once again.

Friends and Soul Mates Cycle

(Continue your tape here.)

Sometimes when you're walking
in the woods or at a beach,
in a store or on a street,
there comes a person who looks familiar.
You look to remember from where or when,
and you know the two of you should meet,
simply because you appear to be old friends.
It's something in his walk
or. . .in her glance;
the gentleness of hand,
or the smiling glow that never ends.

There seems to be rekindled,
deep within, a bubbling joy. . .
surfacing through your breast,

as if there's a surprise coming,
a gift of the universe.

You may find yourself wanting
to embrace this person,
to kiss a cheek
or hold a hand, squeezing tightly,
as if the slight pressure
might push to the surface of your mind
the reasons for this reunion.

When you feel this warm glow,
know then
that you have experienced time
with a special friend.
Know that you've been together
many times before,
meeting in the joy of knowledge,
in the fulfilling of purpose,
in the continuity of life.

And even though your bodies
are temples in different forms,
you recognize the glow.
Now you can see clearly,
and that's a good sign.

This meeting lights the candles
of your mind
and, with clear memory,
past hopes and promises
are surfacing,
reminding you of the reasons you've come
and the work that must be done.

You're fulfilling life's purpose
with each and every one
of the soul friends.

At times the picture clears.
Relieved, you weep for joy.
After all the years,
past becomes present;

and, as you delight in the memory,
you can open doors,
laying the scrolls on the altar of your light.

It doesn't matter
if you speak aloud;
the communication has
already been made.
You've found the remembering to be fun,
the work to be more like a child's game.

The work is in the remembering itself. . .
that's all. . .
the seeing of souls
in all kinds of clothes.
Spread the light of your joy
over and around,
blessing these soul mates,
always recalling the love and fulfillment shared.

Bathe in the glow you've rekindled.
Shower light all around,
even on the place where he is,
on the path where she walks,
on the past you've shared,
and in the present you are now meeting.

Know that you are always
sharing this communion,
and you can simply remember,
in order to fulfill your purpose
and be part of the blessed communion.
Be thankful for soul mates.
And, as you are being thankful,
know that you are clearing a path for all friends.

And some day, as you stand in the woods
or on a beach,
in a store or on a street,
and feel a shower of light, love, and fulfillment
encircle your being,
realize that someone has opened a door

and seen *you,* as before,
recalling you as a friend, a soul friend.

Carry the joy of family,
an emblem that your cup is full
and that you are holding hands,
across dimensions of time,
over hills where a warm sun rises
to meet and join with the glow you rekindle.
Each time you say "hello,"
opening your heart and mind and recognizing a friend.

(Complete your tape with the wake-up procedure.)

NOTE: This is *definitely* a right-brain, feminine cycle. Therefore, some men cannot relate to it just as some women cannot relate to some of the strong left-brain, masculine cycles. Yet I feel it does have a place in this book. So please check with others who have used it before dismissing it.

30   CHAKRA ATTUNEMENT

This cycle is designed as an attunement of the seven spiritual centers in your body. In the East, these spiritual centers are called the chakras, and they relate to the endocrine system (or ductless glands) of the physical body. These neurohormonal energy centers include the pituitary, pineal, thyroid, thymus, adrenals, cells of Leydig, and the gonads.

These centers, which relate to vibrational levels of energy that connect the psychic with the physical, are like doors within you that open and close. Your psychic life may flow abundantly or it can be stagnant.

This cycle uses the vibration of the white light to help open and attune your energy centers. Researchers in photobiology (the study of how light affects animals and plants) are discovering new connections among light, color, and health.

Originally developed as an interpretive self-exploration exercise, this is a delightful self-discovery cycle. In no way, though, should it be considered a definitive or final word on the endocrine system. It is a cycle simply to be enjoyed.

Chakra Attunement Cycle

(Continue your tape here.)

Perhaps you are aware that you are becoming deeply centered. In a few minutes you can begin a series of exercises for understanding better your internal energy centers, the endocrine system of your body. You can mentally attune yourself to this ductless gland system, the most protected system in your body. If you take a deep breath and look inward, deep within yourself, you can imagine your consciousness entering into you. Turn inward and mentally look around within yourself. Venture inside your own body. (Pause)

As you begin this awareness exercise, you may sense or feel or see or hear, or have other intuitive abilities. You can perceive your neurohormonal energy centers in the very core of your physical body. The reason they are the most protected is because this is the seat of your real essence, the very center of your being, the source that is the eternal you. And notice that the energy field of each chakra is alive, pulsating and in motion.

Now, near the center of your head, visualize or sense a clear bright white light. Picture this light as your pituitary gland; this is your superconsciousness. Its vibration is as Jupiter, a beneficial and expanding influence, a giver of life. Perceive this light as a small light bulb aglow with radiant energy. This is the sacred door to spiritual strength, to idealism, and perfection. (Pause)

Now, back and higher in your head, sense a small gland about the size of the tip of your baby finger. Imagine this as a tiny bulb aglow with a vivid light. Perceive this white light as your pineal gland. This is commonly called the third eye or the eye of wisdom. As you send healing attunement to this area, watch the light become brighter. Its energy vibration is as Mercury; it rules intuition, insight, and your spiritual understanding. (Pause)

As you move to your neck and throat area, you can sense a strong white light emanating there. This is your thyroid, ruled by Uranus, with a vibration of change, genius, and inspiration. As you attune your thyroid and parathyroids, the light grows brighter. This is the receptive light of faith, adaptability and freedom—and a special balancing point of your being. (Pause)

Now, going to the thymus in your mid-chest, sense a vibrant white light that is alive with energy, for this is the center of your nervous system. Here is light for going and growing—it is the builder of order and regeneration. The thymus is commonly called the heart chakra, and you are opening this door to unconditional and non-judgmental love. And because it is influenced by Venus, its vibration is sensitive, beautiful, and loving. Thank your thymus, for it determines the energy supply of your body, and let the light shine brighter. (Pause)

You can continue moving to the upper abdomen, near your stomach, to the solar plexus chakra, the adrenals. You can envision a bright white glow of optimism and inspiration. This is the center of awakening creativity, and, because it is influenced by Mars, it is also the door of your strength. The adrenals are your protection and drive. From here come bursts of high-energy adrenalin. Attune this center and feel its strong vibration. (Pause)

You can now go to your next chakra or energy center located in the lower abdomen. This is called the cells of Leydig. Visualize this area aglow with brilliant white light. Here is the light of wisdom shining with vitality, giving and growing. The cells of Leydig are also called the seat of the soul, for it is here that your sealed memory is stored. Neptune—imaginative and mysterious—watches over this area. The white light becomes as a bright flame, an eternal flame of life, guiding personal expression and positive sensuality. (Pause)

Now you can continue to your reproductive center, the gonads, the generative organs of life. Feel the strong white light of high energy and positive passion. This is the source—the beginning, passion, and action. This center is ruled by Saturn—ego and worldly unions. This is the chakra of new life and the continuity of life. Here is the life force and creative fire. (Pause)

Allow the universal white light to brightly flood into your soul in full vibration. Enjoy this attunement, this oneness, this balance. The more you experience, the more you will understand; and the more you understand, the more will be revealed unto you. And as you ask, so shall it be given. And you are given an opportunity for thanksgiving; thank your body, thank your mind, and thank your spirit for this attunement.

(Complete your tape with the wake-up procedure.)

31   HEALING SOUND

This last cycle is presented in its entirety, combined with "Entering Self-Hypnosis I" and the "Wake-Up Procedure." The purpose for this particular presentation is to clarify the process of making your own tape. The steps are simply divided by three stars (* * *). As you are reading the material into your cassette recorder, you do not necessarily need to pause—each step automatically goes into the next one.

The Healing Sound Cycle is similar in some ways to the Song of Life Cycle—both were designed by women musicians who are also knowledgeable about the healing aspects of sound. Healing comes in many ways and in many forms. One of the most innovative is sound. You can enjoy healing sound, not only for the patterns of harmony or song but for the sounds of nature as well. As you flow in the fullness of life, listen to all things happening.

Although still in its infancy, sound therapy may become a major healing art of the future. Just as you tune a musical instrument, so can you attune yourself to the healing principle of life. If you play a musical instrument, you may wish to play some favorite background music for this tape. After you have read these cycles, it is hoped you will be inspired to *write your own.*

Healing Sound Cycle (Complete)

(Start recording your tape.)

Breathe deeply and smoothly for a few minutes. (Pause) You can keep your eyes open for a minute, and you can look either forward or upward. You don't have to look at anything specific, but just look either forward or upward. I am going to count down from ten to one, and with every descending number slowly blink your eyes. Slowly close and then open your eyes, as in slow motion, with every number. Ten. . .nine. . . eight. . .seven. . .six. . .five. . .four. . .three. . .two. . . and one. Now you can close your eyes and you can keep them closed. I will explain what that was for and why you did that.

That was just to relax your eyelids. And right now in your eyelids there is probably a feeling of relaxation, perhaps a comfortable tired feeling, or a pleasant heavy sensation. Whatever the feeling is right now in your eyelids, simply allow that feeling to multiply, to magnify, and to become greater. Allow your eyelids to become totally and pleasantly relaxed. This is something you do; nobody else can do this for you. You are the one who does it.

Now take your time and completely and pleasantly relax your eyelids. And, as you relax your eyelids, you can allow that feeling of relaxation that is now in your eyelids to flow outward in all directions, as in imaginary waves or ripples. Allow a feeling of relaxation to go outward to the entire facial area. Just think about relaxing the face. Allow the relaxation to go outward to the entire head area. Just think about relaxing the head. Enjoy the relaxation going to the neck and to the shoulders, down the arms and into the hands. Welcome a wonderful feeling of relaxation going down the entire body to the legs, to the feet, all the way out to the toes; completely and pleasantly relaxing the entire body. And you slow down a little bit. Allow yourself to slow down just a little bit. Later, as we go along, you can slow down a little bit more.

Don't worry about any little movement in your eyelids. That is called rapid eye movement and is a perfectly normal and natural part of this experience. It will pass very quickly. And, in a moment, I am going to count downward once again from ten to one. This time, as you hear every descending number, just feel yourself slow down a little bit more with every number. At the number one, you can enter your own natural level of relaxation. I will count rapidly now: Ten, nine, eight, seven, six, five, four, three, two, one.

You are now at your own natural level of relaxation. And from this level, you may move to any other level with full awareness and function at will. You are completely aware at every level of your mind even though your body may feel asleep. You can accept or reject anything which is given to you. You are in complete control. At this level, or at any other level, you can give yourself positive mental suggestions— suggestions that your inner mind can accept and act upon in a positive manner—suggestions that are designed for your success—to achieve your goals and ideals.

See yourself relaxed in mind and in body. This is
something that you want; it is here and it is now. As
you take a deep breath, you can enter a deeper and
healthier level of mind—more in perfect harmony,
more centered and balanced—with every breath you
take.

* * *

Now that you are in
your favorite place of relaxation,
just imagine that you can begin
to hear music in the background—
perhaps from an orchestra
or from a band
or a single instrument.
Simply allow music—
any kind of music—
to form in the background of your mind.

Possibly without even choosing
a particular song or tune,
just allow yourself to simply have the idea
of music.
Then, in your bountiful, creative imagination
hear a comforting,
pleasant sound—
floating along—
finding its way to you;
soft music becoming more full and more complete.
Simply imagine that this pleasant, relaxing sound
is filling the place you have created.
And, as your place is filled, this sound of music
floats over and around your being.
It caresses and comforts you,
like a gentle massage;
it heals and soothes you.
The sound of music brings you joy.
Welcome this wave of music with open arms,
ready to receive the comfort and lightness it brings.
As it floats over and around,

caressing and comforting you,
you feel lighter, happier, more fulfilled, more whole.
Welcome the healing music floating through the open
doors of your mind, filling all parts—
in, around, and through—
waves of gentle sound, universal sound,
a healing caress.

You can continue to float on these waves and barely
notice that the sound of the orchestra
or band is far away,
perhaps in another time or place,
but that one tone of the music
has remained with you.

This soft, low vibration
is something like the humming sound
that you might find yourself making at one time
or another;
perhaps you did this as a child.
This is the tone that has remained with you.
It doesn't matter what the exact tone or note is;
the only importance is that it is your special vibration.
You have welcomed this hum, this soundwave,
into your being.
You are doing very well.
The tone is part of you.
The vibration is the same as your vibration;
the same pulse, the same flowing wave,
because the music and you are one.
You are the pulse.
You are the sound.
You are in harmony.

Know that each of us,
every being in every dimension,
has a unique rhythm or vibration.
Everyone and everything has its own pulse-beat,
its own vibration, its own soundwave,
its own musical note.
And, as your wave or tone comes to you,

so you—in just being—
send that tone or wave back out
to meet and greet others.
These waves, our waves,
travel the area around us and vibrate outward,
with rhythm.
This is happening even now.
This is the music of the spheres.

Every being in every dimension
is part of this flowing river of sound.
Tones of healing vibrations merge,
join hands, and follow the flow.
Feel this joining with joy and know that,
as you clasp hands,
the love and healing
are increased
each and every time.
As you float along,
you can recognize, as in a pattern,
an eventual meeting-place,
where all tones merge and vibrations meet.
With each individual note,
your special note,
your special tone,
you follow this flow to return to the center.
Your sound has traveled this path before,
reaching you, teaching you, healing you, attuning you.

Recognize your melody
in the light of the dawn.
Welcome harmony in the breath of the morn.
Accept your sound from every source—
floating on the leaves of trees,
in the wind on your cheek,
in the joyful sounds and symbols of spring,
or in meditative peace.
Realize your tone in everything you see, hear, and do.
Return the love and healing strength,
knowing that these wonderful benefits
will be shared by all,

by all who may reach out and touch you
along the way.
Feel joy in sharing the gifts of the universe
with all life in every dimension.
Experience rejuvenation in knowing
that these healing sounds,
these caressing vibrations,
are available always.
All you need do is simply accept them.

Be thankful for your place in the Plan
of the grand universe, the living cosmos.
Realize that your tone, your sound, your attunement,
is always clear and true.

* * *

Your conscious mind may forget to remember all that
you accomplished here today. But your subconscious
mind always remembers. It is already acting upon
these suggestions and these visualized images in a
positive manner. Benefit—success—can come at any
time. It can come back with you now, or you can
experience it in due time. And, in a little while, when
you return, you will feel just wonderful. But before you
come back here, be aware that you can drift back
clear-headed—that you will be wide awake, refreshed,
and happy.

I will count from one to ten; at the count of ten, you
will open your eyes, be alert, energized, and feeling
fine—feeling better than before. I will count now:
one. . .two. . .coming out slowly. . .three. . .four. . .
coming up now. . .five. . .six. . .feel the circulation
returning and equalizing. . .seven. . .eight. . .
awakening your full potential with perfect equilibrium
and normalization throughout your being. . .nine. . .
ten. Open your eyes. . .wide awake and feeling great.

(Your tape is now complete and ready to enjoy.)

THE WORK OF EDGAR CAYCE TODAY

The Association for Research and Enlightenment, Inc. (A.R.E.®), is a membership organization founded by Edgar Cayce in 1931.

• 14,256 Cayce readings, the largest body of documented psychic information anywhere in the world, are housed in the A.R.E. Library/Conference Center in Virginia Beach, Virginia. These readings have been indexed under 10,000 different topics and are open to the public.

• An attractive package of membership benefits is available for modest yearly dues. Benefits include: a bi-monthly magazine; lessons for home study; a lending library through the mail, which offers collections of the actual readings as well as one of the world's best parapsychological book collections, names of doctors or health care professionals in your area.

• As an organization on the leading edge in exciting new fields, A.R.E. presents a selection of publications and seminars by prominent authorities in the fields covered, exploring such areas as parapsychology, dreams, meditation, world religions, holistic health, reincarnation and life after death, and personal growth.

• The unique path to personal growth outlined in the Cayce readings is developed through a worldwide program of study groups. These informal groups meet weekly in private homes.

• A.R.E. maintains a visitors' center where a bookstore, exhibits, classes, a movie, and audiovisual presentations introduce inquirers to concepts from the Cayce readings.

• A.R.E. conducts research into the helpfulness of both the medical and nonmedical readings, often giving members the opportunity to participate in the studies.

For more information and a color brochure, write or phone:

A.R.E., Dept. C., P.O. Box 595
Virginia Beach, VA 23451, (804) 428-3588